The iN Crowd

Life. Legacy. Leadership

I0152470

Kahlil Carter "Coach S.W.A.A.G."

ISBN: 979-8-218-41589-1

Library of Congress Control Number: (if needed for libraries)

_____ Publishing date: 04/15/2024

(Publisher Logo)

Cover Design by Michael Scott, MASgraphicarts.com

Dedication

This book is dedicated to my heavenly friend and former teammate, Brandon Burlsworth. Thank you for showing me the heart and resilience of a true champion and Christian. Your story was truly an Inspiration to me and countless other walk-ons who trusted the process and the sport of football. I am forever changed by our friendship and your impact on me and our beloved sport. See you at the crossroads my friend.

Table of Content

Warm-Up

Whether or not you've ever pursued the dream of becoming a professional athlete, there are some real-life lessons that go beyond the game and seep into our everyday existence. You know, the daily grind we all face day after day, year after year. If you've ever kicked a ball or played any sport at all, you'll relate to the ups and downs of my journey. And even if not, well, I'm sure life's given you its fair share of those rollercoaster moments. Either way, my story is about winning, losing, adapting, transitioning, overcoming, and everything **in** between.

In these pages, you'll learn from my personal stories and the lessons I've learned. You'll learn how to tackle life's greatest obstacles and lead a successful, purpose-driven life. This book also dives into the art of transition, whether it be switching jobs, hopping from one career to another, or taking the plunge from the nine-to-five grind to full-time entrepreneurship. It can even be moving from one relationship status to another. From being single to being married to becoming parents, and any other transition you can think of.

But here's the thing - I'm not going to hand it to you in a tidy package of bullet points and principles because that's not how life is. Life can get messy. It can take you on wild highs and knock the wind out of you with its devastating lows. It's a crazy ride of experiences and challenges, and I'm here to unravel it for you.

The lessons I've gathered along the way are woven through each story, disappointment, and victory. By sharing my personal narrative, the neighborhood and family dynamics I grappled with in my formative years, and the wisdom accrued during my athletic and coaching career, I aim to convey a powerful message. My hope is that you'll recognize how the battles, challenges, and triumphs in your own life serve a powerful purpose to demonstrate that your dreams are within reach through unwavering determination and hard work. What seems impossible can indeed become possible. God has the ability to take your chaos and transform it into a profound testimony of His grace and mercy.

Now, let's talk about "The **iN** Crowd," the title of thisbook. Although it's just a play on words with the proverbial **"in crowd,"** the concept goes beyond semantics. It signifies inclusion, being part of a particular group, societal element, or status. Reflecting on my life, I've come to realize that I've never truly been part of the **"in crowd."** I wasn't the celebrated high school athlete, nor the favored oldest son who received all the privileges and responsibilities, nor some renowned college athlete with a scholarship; I never got any of that. Even after experiencing measurable success and earning the spotlight on the football field for a significant amount of time, I still felt like an outsider.

In a way, my life has been a continual journey of striving to be part of the conversation, to be relevant, and to utilize that relevance to advocate for God and convey the keys to success to others. I excelled in my profession for a good while, but when I achieved what I thought was the pinnacle of my career, it didn't really last long. But this only compelled me to explore new avenues and find other ways to reinvent myself.

If you're an athlete, my objective with this book is to impart wisdom about the challenges of a life in professional football, while also offering insights into how to conduct yourself within the system. I've secured jobs based on my qualifications, kept them through sheer dedication, late hours, and innovative thinking, and regrettably lost opportunities by failing to count the cost of my words and actions.

Throughout these pages, I want people to know Kahlil, the man, and separate him from KC, the player, or Coach Carter. At my core, I'm a man who loves and serves his family, and that's who I want to be, now and forever. The roles of coach and player are like characters played by an actor in a movie, and it must be said that separating these roles hasn't always been my forte. I've often struggled to leave behind my player or coaching hat when I'm not on the field or at work. But regardless of who I was then, my ultimate aspiration is to be known as a man dedicated to serving God, rather than just being the guy who blows the whistle and tries to win championships. Don't get me wrong; I still want to be recognized as a goal-oriented sports professional with a love for the game and a relentless pursuit of goals. What I want is to be more than just a coach who's in it for the job.

I thank and praise God for His grace and mercy, for the ability to live, make mistakes, and fix mistakes, because a lot of people don't get the chance to tell their story. It's a privilege not everyone is granted, and some depart from this world with their untold tales still buried within them. My aspiration is to reciprocate God's benevolence by expressing my profound appreciation for the countless opportunities He's afforded me over the years. And finally, I'm grateful for the fact that He has granted me the chance to share my narrative with anyone who is willing to listen.

Now, are *you* listening?
Let's *go!*

Pre-Game: Faith, Family, Football

"What then shall we say to these things? If God is for us, who can be against us? He who did not spare His own Son, but delivered Him up for us all, how shall He not with Him also freely give us all things? Who shall bring a charge against God's elect? It is God who justifies. Who is he who condemns? It is Christ who died, and furthermore is also risen, who is even at the right hand of God, who also makes intercession for us. Who shall separate us from the love of Christ? Shall tribulation, or distress, or persecution, or famine, or nakedness, or peril, or sword? As it is written: "For Your sake, we are killed all day long;

We are accounted as sheep for the slaughter."

Pre-Game - Part I

Back in the mid-90s, when I was donning the jersey for the University of Arkansas football team as a walk-on, Tupac Shakur released an album entitled "Me Against the World," featuring a song where he illustrated the struggles faced by black men in America. Originally born on the East Coast but residing in the South, I could connect with some of the sentiments he expressed. Among the tracks on this album was one that quickly became iconic-Dear Mama. Here was T upac, pouring his heart out about the immense love, respect, and gratitude he had for his mother. It was emotional stuff, and it struck a particular chord with me, because I had similar feelings for my mom.

It's a recurring theme in the lives of many successful people, be they entertainers or athletes, to attribute a significant portion of their achievements to their mothers. I'm no exception.

My mom was, and still is, my hero.

I wish you could meet my mom. Her name is Linda, and in just a few moments of conversation, you'd grasp the remarkable, clairvoyant spirit that emanated from her, complementing her soulful voice and gracious demeanor. My mother, a student who consistently earned straight-A's throughout high school and college, personified what it meant to be a young, successful African-American single parent.

Standing at a modest five feet and two inches, my mom's milk-chocolate-hued skin and amber-brown eyes served as the canvas for her infectious smile. When she smiles, the room comes to life, much like the way a Christmas tree lights up in a darkened living room. In the '70s, she sported a meticulously styled afro, and it was a regular occurrence around our home to witness her getting her groove on to the soulful tunes of Gerald Levert, Luther Vandross, and Whitney Houston. As the '80s rolled in, it was all about the slow jams. My mom's a woman brimming with spirit, possessing a serious love for football. I've lost count of the numerous sporting events she took to during those days. The only downside was when she insisted on packing lunches instead of letting us indulge in fast food. Our noses would regularly wrinkle at the pungent smell and taste of warm bologna and cheese. We grimaced whenever we had to eat those suckers.

Mom had a look that could freeze lava if we misbehaved, and she never failed to issue a verbal warning before we left home. She'd say, "Now, Kahlil-" Or, addressing all of us at once while quoting Bill Cosby, "I brought you all into this world, and I'll take you *out*" She was a fair disciplinarian, but we knew well enough that she could unleash some real wrath when necessary. Mom didn't *ta.keno mess,* and no one understood this better than us *kids!*

She was extremely meticulous about nearly everything, especially particular about how others treated us. Once again, mom didn't *ta.keno mess* from others either.

At that time, the immensely popular show was "Wonder Woman," starring Lynda Carter. Well, my mom's name at that time was Linda Carter, and you couldn't convince me that my mom wasn't the epitome of a black Wonder Woman. She managed everything for us without a husband or boyfriend in the picture. As I mentioned earlier, my mom remains my hero, my Wonder Woman. Whether it was shoes, clothes, or extra school supplies, Mom consistently demonstrated our importance and value to her. Through an incredible amount of hard work and unwavering attention to us, she provided the best possible care for my siblings and me, ensuring that we lived just as well as anyone else in the projects.

I remember how I couldn't wait for Christmas to arrive because I knew the day would be brimming with food, festivities, and the annual traditions mom had established from the beginning. She also celebrated our birthdays in grand style with cakes, gifts, balloons, and loads of fun. Often, all of us would pile into the 1976 copper-colored Ford Mustang we affectionately named "Penny" and embark on family adventures to theme parks and other exciting destinations. All in all, my mother could have easily won the Mother of the Year award multiple times over. That was just her way - always prioritizing her children's needs.

Beyond her role as a mother, my mom was socially active and exceptionally aware, a groundbreaking African-American woman. She was the first African-American female to be appointed as the Director of Admissions for the University of Arkansas Medical School. I distinctly recall feeling immensely proud of her, but honestly, nothing about my mother surprised me because, in my eyes, she was capable of anything; as far as I was concerned, she could simply walk in and secure any job she wanted.

I've gleaned no small number of life lessons from my mom, many of which continue to guide me to this day. One of the most significant lessons I learned from her was the importance of hard work in achieving success. Thanks to her example and my own innate drive, I've always known what it takes to position myself for success in anything I pursue. I inherited that from my mom's example, maybe even from a touch of her DNA, too! Whenever my mom worked in corporate America in some capacity, I stood tall and held my head high when I entered the doors of the companies where she was employed in downtown Washington, DC.

I'd think to myself, *Mom must be incredibly important to work in the heart of our nation's capital!*

***

We were latchkey kids.

At six, seven, and even eight years old, my brothers and I would let ourselves in after school. We'd complete our homework, make our beds, do the dishes, and change from our school clothes into play clothes, all without our mom being present. Of course, we had vigilant neighbors who watched over us, adhering to the adage, "It takes a village to raise your children."

Back then, life was much simpler. We spent the entire day outdoors, crafting bows and arrows, fashioning slingshots from rubber bands and tree branches, and playing until exhaustion forced us to drag our feet back home. Every evening, when mom returned, she would ask, "Who won today?" This was her way of learning about our day and assessing whether we'd found reasons to celebrate victory in life. We always felt like winners because she was a master of optimism. She frequently reminded us that, as black males, we must find victory in everything we do, as life's challenges often push us to contemplate failure.

"Focus on victory," she would tell us, "For victory leads to heaven."

I can't muster the words to adequately express the immense positive influence my mom had on my life during my adolescent years. The years between 1976 and 1987 were incredibly tumultuous, with America facing many challenges, such as wars, economic recession, and the emergence of drugs and HIV. During this period of serious socio-economic upheaval, my mother firmly guided my young mind and character, instilling values that have remained with me throughout the years. Despite her later struggles with sobriety, my mom singlehandedly provided abundant nurturing for a growing young man, nourishing my spirit for life. I will forever be grateful for what she instilled in me.

I recall that during my middle school years, we were firmly in the lower middle class because my mother was in the middle of switching jobs. For school, I received only one pair of shoes and two or three pairs of pants. My brothers and I did not have the finest clothes, and designer clothing was out of the question, which left me feeling somewhat deprived at times. The privileges that well-off kids with good grades enjoyed seemed out of reach. This had a significant impact on my self-image because I lacked

9

trendy clothes and nice possessions. My closest friends had Jordans,

Nikes, and other top-brand items, while I had generic shoes. I was fortunate if even one of those pairs survived from the previous year; the other pair was always something affordable and ordinary, like a twenty-dollar pair of moccasins or the like. The truth is, I ended up wearing those moccasins for nearly half the year, despite them ripping and tearing along the seams. They weren't suitable for playing basketball during recess or running around outside. My self-esteem hit an all-time low, and I felt economically disadvantaged in comparison to everyone around me.

Much of my adolescence was spent in Landover, Maryland, in a housing project called Cherry Hills. When we first moved there, it was a solidly middle-class neighborhood with numerous families, and clean, new playgrounds and buildings. Over time, though, drug dealers, addicts, and gang members started making themselves at home in the neighborhood, and as a result, the crime rate rose, and the neighborhood headed into decline. Shattered storefronts, trashy sidewalks, shady people in dark, and an abundance of car thefts started to make the neighborhood unsafe. It felt as though we were growing up in a war zone. You name it, and it was happening there!

The corrosive influences of our environment began to weigh on all of us, but it was my eldest brother, Aaron, who felt the impact the most. I was his steadfast sidekick, and together, we began a life of petty theft from stores, apartment break-ins, and the reckless thrill of joyriding in stolen cars, all before we even turned

13. My mother had a sense that we were getting ourselves in trouble, but she was determined to keep us from falling into the clutches of the juvenile detention system. With this resolve, she made a pivotal decision: moving us out of that increasingly messed- up neighborhood and into our first rented house. This house was a substantial upgrade from the cramped two-bedroom apartment we'd called home. For a single mother with three sons, three bedrooms felt like a palace. Our new neighborhood sprawled out before us, and while it still had its share of troubles, the shift in our environment altered our lives forever. My mom possessed an innate intuition akin to a radar. She saved us countless times.

While caring for us, my mother was also always striving to improve our circumstances. Throughout my middle school years, I vividly remember her struggle to find a career path that matched her education and passion, one that would offer better opportunities. It was during this pursuit of more lucrative and fulfilling work that she approached us one day with a bold announcement: "Hey kids, we're moving to Arkansas!" At first, I thought she was taking an insane risk, but history has shown that she made wise decisions. We trusted her judgment. I was just around IO years old at the time, and the notion of relocating to a distant city filled me with fear. I suppose the thought of being alone in an unfamiliar place was what gnawed at me, giving rise to uncertainty and doubt.

Yet, we gathered our lives, bid farewells to the family, and embarked on a journey into uncharted territory. We had no idea what to expect, but we were together, and that was enough.

We eventually moved to Pine Bluff, Arkansas, one of the poorest cities in America per capita. We settled in a part of town where many middle-class families resided, so we felt safe and even experienced an improvement in our living conditions. However, we soon realized that the Jim Crow South was markedly different and less progressive compared to Washington, D.C., and Maryland. It was just us as it had *always* been...just us.

Arkansas felt like an entirely different world, a vast distance away from the familiar, and the transition to Southern culture from the East Coast was harsh and jarring. To our dismay, it also turned out that gang activity, drug-related issues, and tragic incidents were all too common in this new environment. It was disheartening, to say the least. The Pine Bluff neighborhood started much like Cherry Hills in Maryland, solidly middle-class. However, over time, it transformed into a hub for gang activity and drug-related problems. Shabby houses with peeling paint, shattered windows, crumbling sidewalks, and aging, worn-out chairs and sofas gracing creaking porches were stark reminders of the poverty we encountered. My initial perception of Arkansas was rather one-sided, even though there were more affluent neighborhoods on the other side of town. In that neighborhood, some of my friends lost their lives, their freedom, and their innocence.

Looking back, I often thought that growing up in Washington, D.C., might have been a better option for us, especially when comparing it to life in the South. Nevertheless, at the time, I had to follow my mother's lead.

Shortly after our move to Arkansas, my mother made a wonderful decision: she married her longtime close friend and the best stepfather a child could ask for, Thorn. Thorn was a remarkable man *who* had been a part of our lives for over a decade as a close family friend. He was the kind of man *who* treated us like his own children, and I absolutely loved him. Tall and bespectacled, he was an honest, hardworking, fair, family-oriented, and incredibly handy individual. He was Clark Kent-humble and unassuming. Thorn taught us the essentials of manhood, from tying a tie to fixing a flat tire, changing an alternator, and mowing the grass. Along with his own children, a son and a daughter, we all lived together in a comfortable three-bedroom house, while my stepsister resided with her mother in Chicago. Thorn's presence provided an additional source of income in our household, improving the prospects for all of us.

Our family's fortunes continued to rise as we eventually moved to Little Rock, the capital of Arkansas. We settled into a spacious two-story, four-bedroom house on the west side of Little Rock, which felt like a mansion to us. The neighborhood was charming, with beautiful houses, parks, and friendly people. Although we didn't own the house, my mother and Thom worked tirelessly to provide a nurturing environment for our success. The sacrifices we all made were paying off, and each of the kids was better off for it.

Around this time, my mother's career began to soar. She advanced from Minority Director to becoming the Director of Student Admissions at the University of Arkansas Medical School. Meanwhile, Thom received a promotion to Regional Director, overseeing multiple McDonald's locations. In just a matter of years, we transitioned from middle-class to upper-middle-class. During those times, fast food became a regular part of our lives. Thom instilled in me the values of being a good person, working a respectable job, taking care of family, attending church, and practicing honesty. He demonstrated that an honest day's work held more value than any amount of money. Both he and my mother laid the groundwork for me to be **iNcomparable,** both on the field and in life.

Pre-Game - Part II

When I turned fourteen, something ignited within me; I yearned for better things. I **never** wanted to endure the embarrassment of those worn-out moccasins I wore during middle school again. And so, in the summer of I 990, I decided to take action.

My mom had recently secured a position at the University of Arkansas Medical School, and she arranged for me to work there. Her intention was to teach me the ways of working in an office, and how to conduct myself around professionals, and she could use the extra help with filing and general office tasks. Back then, the minimum wage was a meager $4.25, but I was fortunate to make about $8.60 an hour-and so, needless to say, I came into work with a bounce in my step and a smile on my face, all while trying to act as professionally as a fourteen-year-old boy could. I kept working every year, even after I became a professional athlete. That lesson of working to provide stuck with me forever.

Additionally, thanks to my stepfather, Thom, who now was the Regional Manager of two McDonald's, I had the opportunity to work intermittently at one of his stores from the age of fifteen until I left for college, even during winter and spring breaks. I advanced to become a crew trainer and one of the most highly regarded non-managerial employees. Whether it was running the drive-through, cooking, or working the front counter, I could get it done. I was stationed at a two-story McDonald's and took pride in maintaining impeccable standards from top to bottom. My time at the University of Arkansas Medical School had prepared me to interact with a diverse clientele, including the most professional and urban of customers.

During Bill Clinton's presidential campaign, I worked at McDonald's along his campaign trail, and I had the privilege of serving him breakfast a few times. My status as a Regional Manager's son made me one of the few employees entrusted with this responsibility. McDonald's was more than just a job; it was a source of valuable skills. I learned how to operate a cash register, perfect customer service, manage inventory, and even supervise a team, albeit as a junior supervisor. Instead of roaming the streets, I was contributing to the success of a business. It instilled in me confidence, responsibility, and the sheer value of a clear plan. As Benjamin Franklin once wisely said, "Those who fail to plan, plan to fail."

***

Earlier, I mentioned how my mother was and remains my hero-but of course, she still had her imperfections. Like any human being, she faced numerous challenges in life, including a battle with substance abuse. Though she's now completely sober, her addiction cost her the job at the University of Arkansas Medical School. This difficult period coincided with the dissolution of her marriage and the rise of our family's struggles. She made the decision to relocate to Maryland to be near her family and support system, taking my younger brother Randii with her. I wasn't **in** favor of this move, for I had a gut feeling that her substance abuse would negatively impact Randii-and it did.

At that time, I was just 20 years old and had recently refocused on returning to the University of Arkansas football team. I found myself faced with a monumental decision: to stay and play or go back to Maryland with my mother. This choice weighed heavily on my mind, but with no clear guidance, I chose to return to the

University of Arkansas in 1996. My intention was to complete what I had started and play for the Razorback football team.

That decision ended up being one of the biggest regrets in my life. In retrospect, I should have probably gone back to Maryland with my mom and brother. Mom needed a man in the house with her, not my I 4-year-old younger brother. I might have considered transferring to the University of Maryland, or a division IAA school, or even a historically black college in the area. I've often wondered if that path might have offered a better chance of making it professionally, given the proximity of NFL teams.

In any case, I should have been there for my mom. I struggled to understand and empathize with her substance abuse, her depression, her guilt, and how her illness affected her. As an adult, I now understand her struggle better, and better grasp how people can get caught in their pain and hurt. The need to escape the past and the present, feelings of inadequacy that contribute to the disease, and a perceived helplessness in breaking free. I consider my decision a missed opportunity to support my mom, a choice that my older brother probably also regrets. Neither of us went with her, and in that moment. .. we failed her.

Now, my older brother had his own challenges. When I talk about his involvement in gangs and criminal activities, I keep in mind that Aaron experienced the same pitfalls as I did with having no father in the picture. He was plagued by some of the same demons that haunted me, so I'm sensitive to the fact that he was making poor decisions without the benefit of our father being around, but at the same time, that's who he was. I don't want to portray him as the worst of the worst, because he simply wasn't. Nonetheless, he was notorious for the things he did on the streets. His reputation and activity out there probably saved me some major headaches, in fact. People in my neighborhood and school were literally afraid to cross me for fear of offending him. I was protected by all the biggest and most dangerous of them all. Our uncanny resemblance immediately triggered a familiarity with DC, the name he had become well-known by. Everyone recognized me for his reputation and exploits in the streets of Little Rock.

It's terribly unfortunate that many men of color sometimes veer down the wrong path. Whether it's the difficulty of a particular high school class, a breakup with a girlfriend, or a challenging family situation, some let these minor setbacks derail them instead of learning from them. I'm grateful that I chose to build upon my small victories, not dwelling on the obstacles or the negativity that tried to attach itself to me. To me, failure isn't a permanent state, but rather a temporary or momentary setback. I firmly believe that if you don't plan to succeed, you can't succeed in your plan. I've often been misunderstood, with some mistaking my attitude for arrogance and narcissism. However, my focus has always been on achieving success, not on how to fail. If I do encounter failure, I immediately think about how to bounce back. I always aim for success, and even in the face of failure, I strive to find a way to win.

"Kahlil's strength is his work ethic," Donnell Fletcher, my former teammate at U of A, has said. "I mean, you talk about a guy who on every level was counted out but overcame everything anybody ever put in front of him to continue on and work at his craft and be great, just to try to be great, be better. . .I don't think the word "no" is in his vocabulary, and the word "can't" is *defimi:ely* not in his vocabulary. That is something he doesn't even speak of, so if somebody would try to use that against him, that right there would drive him more than anything else to prove the person wrong."

Donnell's words resonate with me because my relentless attitude can sometimes come across differently to certain people. I've encountered individuals with unique perspectives, and I've been able to appreciate that aspect of them because of the value they bring. When others witness how I bounce back from failure, it might lead them to perceive me as overconfident. But this is who I am, and honestly, I don't even know how to change it. In fact, I'm not sure I want to. People often tell me, "I love the way you are; you're such a fighter." However, it's worth acknowledging that having that fighting spirit can sometimes lead to internal conflict.

Psychologists often advise that it's essential to be true and authentic to who you are, emphasizing that you're not here to impress anyone else. Yet that does not mean you're not on a self-improvement course, because you're always seeking improvement in one area or another. You must be true to who God intended you to be.

My mother deserves all the credit for humbling our arrogance by holding us accountable and refusing to tolerate any nonsense. This upbringing is, I believe, the foundation of my pursuit of self-confidence. However, I must acknowledge that there are moments when my self-confidence is misconstrued as arrogance. I've found myself at odds with enough people to realize that there may be a part of me still struggling with the desire to be *too much* of something-too *much* like my father, *too much* like my mother, or maybe even *too much* like my stepfather, despite him being a good man. Could it be that I'm trying too hard *not* to resemble him simply because he wasn't extroverted? Somewhere in these questions, I recognize my own responsibility.

I assume responsibility in areas of my life that propel me to the next level, all the while constantly seeking to reinvent myself, even if it carries the risk of losing touch with who I genuinely am. My close friend and former teammate, CFL Hall ofFamer Damon Allen, once shared his perspective, saying, "As a player, listening to Kahlil and his desire, he would always talk about being called the People's Champ. He'd talk about his skill set and the things he could do. While I think it was good for him to have that level of confidence in himself and his abilities, it was, at times, perceived as arrogance or a belief that he was bigger than the team. This perspective probably rubbed some players the wrong way, as they interpreted his comments as selfishness, but I didn't view him as a selfish player at all."

***

My mother instilled a valuable lesson in me as a young black man: she emphasized the importance of both academics and sports as the pathways to success. She would frequently remind me, saying, "Kahlil, you must stay intelligent, obey the law, and go to school." I heeded her advice and made it a point to continue learning and striving for self-improvement.

During my young adult years, I also learned the significance of placing God at the forefront of my life and leaning on Him. However, at one stage in my career, when I was still maturing, I began to place other priorities on par with my faith. This occurred because I lacked proper guidance and support in my spiritual development. There was no one by my side, holding my hand, reading the Bible with me, explaining scriptures, or attending church with me. Young people often make mistakes, but those who remain close to God can avoid some significant pitfalls that others might fall into due to not prioritizing their faith. For young people reading this, and perhaps even those of you who are more seasoned in your spiritual journey, I'd like to emphasize this: Whatever you do, do it to please God. And when you're uncertain, lean even more on God and His Word.

IfI had done that, I believe I would have reached my goals much earlier in life. Perhaps I wouldn't have had a child out of wedlock, and some of the challenges I faced in my adolescence wouldn't haunt me as they do today. Like T upac, I had to deal with gang violence and my mother's substance abuse. But ifI had relied more on God during those years, I might have performed better in school and earned a full-ride scholarship to college. IfI could have a do-over, I would have emphasized academic excellence from an earlier age, and I would have been more faithful to God and more obedient. Even though I wasn't a troublemaker, I wish I could have been extraordinary for God. It is never too late to press the reset button on your spirit, to have a do-over, fixing the things keeping you down.

***

During my young adult years, as I drew closer to my Heavenly Father, I found myself reflecting on the relationship I had with my biological father. My dad was a missing presence in my life, in stark contrast to my mother, who was my hero. If my mom was the hero, my dad seemed to play the role of the anti-hero. He was someone I knew I didn't want to grow up to resemble. He was a great individual in some ways, but not as a father.

His name was Aaron, though he went by the nickname Oma. He practiced the Islamic faith and was deeply rooted in Afro- centric traditions. His lifestyle was best described by the song "Papa Was A Rolling Stone" as he moved through life in a somewhat nomadic manner. Unfortunately, he never seemed to fulfill his true potential, and that frustrated me. My dad was an **incredibly** talented artist, known for his work in the North Carolina area, which often found its way to schools and colleges. However, he seemed to lose his sense of purpose and place in the system. He became very *and-establishment,* refusing to work for any company or entity because of his strong opposition to government and taxation. He chose to stay under the radar to avoid being tracked. This lifestyle had a profound impact on our relationship because his lack of a stable income made him feel like he couldn't provide for us, which brought him great shame. My mother did her best by sending us to spend time with him during the holidays, but it was never enough. What we needed was a father, not just a vacation.

Nonetheless, there are a few positives to my father. I've heard that he was a brilliant artist, both in terms of music and visual arts. He had a dynamic, charismatic personality and treated others with respect and kindness. My cousin once referred to him as his favorite uncle, but personally, I didn't get to know him very well. He was known for his altruism in the community and possessed a gift for inspirational speaking. However, his strong religious and political beliefs seemed to limit his ability to fully utilize these talents. From what I understand, he struggled to reconcile the complicated dynamics between his biological father, mother, and stepfather, an experience that left lasting scars and significantly influenced his idea of fatherhood. I believe that his inability to heal from these wounds played a role in hindering his potential as my father.

The lifestyle he chose led to discord in my entire family, even affecting my own relationship with my children. I have made it my mission to reverse my father's absence from my own life experiences. I tell my kids, "You can achieve anything you can dream of. You have an exceptional gene pool, but you must apply yourself. If you don't, you'll be average." I strive to apply everything I tell my children to my own life. I've worked harder than anyone in my personal circle. During my playing days, I distinguished myself by dedicating my time to running and weightlifting while many of my teammates were content lounging around or frequenting clubs. I'm seriously glad to have inherited my mother's dominant hard-work gene-though I'm not sure just what I inherited from my dad.

In the end, it all came down to the lingering resentment between my mother and father due to their religious differences. Whenever they spoke, there was a palpable anger in his voice; his brows would furrow, and his shoulders would tense up towards his neck. Regrettably, us kids became the unfortunate conduit for expressing that bitterness. I guess I must've inherited that, too.

Pre-Game - Part III

Fast forward to my early twenties, I was just twenty-three when my father passed away. Dealing with his death proved challenging because we had never managed to develop a meaningful, close relationship. This occurred in the year 2000, my first year playing professional football in the inaugural season of the Arena 2 Football League. I was part of my hometown team, the Arkansas Twisters, which was a minor league system of the Arena Football League. One of our final games that season was held in Greensboro, North Carolina, an hour's drive from my family's hometown in Winston-Salem. My mom's family also hailed from Hamlet, North Carolinaf a small town situated about two hours south of both Greensboro and Winston-Salem.

I vividly recall that game in Greensboro. However, it took place while my father was fighting for his life, clinging to life support due to a severe car accident he had been involved in. As the game kicked off, the clock was ticking down on his life. He had been on the road, driving from Winston-Salem to Columbia, South

Carolina, far from my location. I couldn't be with him at the hospital. The news of his accident hit me like a Mike Tyson punch to the gut. I was devastated by the fact that he was dying, or possibly going to die. Regret lingers to this day because I chose to play in that game instead of being by his side. He passed away around ten o'clock that night, while our game started at seven.

Ironically, just two or three weeks before his car accident, I felt an overwhelming urge to call my father. It was as if the Holy Spirit was guiding me to make amends. I picked up the phone and said, "I forgive you for everything that's happened in our lives. I understand that you have your own life, and you are your own man. Despite the fact that my mother was left to raise us on her own, I forgive you." I took a quick breath and continued, 'Tm going to put your four-year-old granddaughter (my eldest daughter) on the phone."

You see, I had always spoken highly of my father to her, because, from an outsider's perspective, my father was an amazing, brilliant, socially conscious man. It's just that he wasn't a great father to me personally. While my dad was on his deathbed, an unexpected turn of events occurred on the football field. In the first quarter, our team's starting quarterback got injured, and I had the most substantial game action of my career up to that point. Although I had only sporadically played before, I was now the star quarterback I had always dreamt of becoming.

Let me tell you, I had the best game of my life during that night in Greensboro. I accumulated about two hundred passing yards, threw three touchdowns, caught a touchdown, and ran for another. I was all over the field, making plays, and all I could think about was that my father's spirit and essence were somehow transferring into me. I felt unstoppable that night. The Greensboro game served as the catalyst that propelled me to the next level. I now knew what true success on the field felt like, and I felt spiritually fortified to move forward.

That night was exceptional in so many ways. My father passed away, I had my best game, and I was playing in my family's hometown with all of them in the stands. During the game, they left when they found out he was dying. At his funeral, my tears flowed like Niagara Falls when I saw my father lying in the casket. Shortly after my dad's passing, my grandfather also left this world.

He was a completely different influence in my life, a strong, un-wavering pillar of a man. He lived a long life marked by activity and consistency. I couldn't bring myself to attend his funeral. After witnessing my father's mortality, I couldn't bear to see my grand-father in that same state. Following my grandfather's passing, my favorite uncle succumbed to pancreatic cancer. Though I attended his funeral, I couldn't bring myself to look at his casket either. The image of these strong, invincible men in my life being defeated by death weighed heavily on my soul.

Now, I look back at these events with a different perspective. I choose to remember them for who they were when they were alive and not for the void their deaths left in my soul. As a young adult, I realized that God was present with me through each of these losses. While the experience of these men's deaths took a toll on me, it served as a transformative journey into manhood.

***

I've had many unique life experiences, both as an individual and alongside my siblings. Education was something our grandmother, Dorothy Graham, helped instill in all of us. However, it saddens me to acknowledge that there has been a recurring theme in my family: a struggle to fully realize our true potential. I personally achieved my goals through relentless dedication. I thank God for inheriting my mom's unwavering drive, magnified to an extraor-dinary level. I inherited her indomitable will, focused energy, relentless drive, and unyielding determination.

I knew I didn't want to follow in my father's footsteps. Instead, I looked up to my older brother, Aaron Jr. I was Aaron Jr.'s shadow, probably up until high school. He introduced me to sports and the unspoken rules of survival in our neighborhood. Both of us were a blend of our father and our mother, and you could say I was a smaller version of him. He shone as the brightest star I had ever seen, excelling in ROTC, football, basketball, social in-teractions, fashion, style, art-you name it. He seemed to be ef-fortlessly talented in everything he did. He had it all. I can still hear Aaron's confident voice as he declared his aspirations of becoming a famous player or a 5-star Army General. He was an exceptional big brother, athletic and intelligent. I was the younger brother trying to keep up, and he set a high bar.

Since we didn't have a father around, Aaron ran our household like a well-oiled machine. He established a merit system, akin to a regiment, where he assigned merits and demerits. If we went against his wishes, we would receive demerits, and if we did as he instructed, we earned merits. Regardless of our personal feelings about Aaron's system, one thing remained consistent: we learned the value of order and respect. We did everything together-practiced karate and ninjitsu, formed a BMX crew, played every sport (with a particular fondness for football), and mastered the timeless art of breakdancing. We embraced the 1980s lifestyle with gusto, and our adventures could have easily been the plot of a movie. We were Wu-Tang-tough young kids from a hostile, challenging neighborhood, surviving the best we could.

My younger brother, Randii, was undeniably bright, surpassing all of us in potential. He shared our name and our Carter values, despite having a different father. We upheld the "brother's keeper" principle. Randii embarked on a college journey, but an acute asthma attack abruptly halted his education, and he never returned.

Randii had consistently been a straight-A student up to high school, but as my mother's substance abuse began to grip her life, I assumed the role of a parent, guiding him through high school and into college. From the earliest of my memories, our mother used to tell us, "I'll be gone one day. You're only going to have each other." Whenever we quarreled, argued, or tussled a bit too vigorously, she'd echo her mantra as only Mama could, "Alright now, when I'm gone, you're only going to have each other." It was this very phrase that kept us tightly bound. To this day, a sense of duty lingers, like an unspoken code of honor. Our brotherhood and camaraderie were forged out of necessity.

However, there's another brother I haven't yet mentioned - the one who never made it.

Prior to my birth, my parents, my mother and father, were expecting a child, and they named him Bosede. Tragically, he didn't survive in the womb. I came into this world as a love child after the loss of Bosede, and as a result, I received an extra measure of my parents' affection. I've always held the belief that Bosede's spirit has been with me throughout my life. I sense his presence, a profound connection that transcends the physical. It's as though his spirit essence transferred to me in that womb, and I often feel like I'm two people in one. Without Bosede's presence, I doubt I would have endured the trials and achieved all that I have. It's almost as if I've had a guardian angel.

The way my parents nurtured me differed from their approach with my older brother, Aaron, and I believe it's because they mourned the loss of Bosede. My mother, in particular, displayed greater affection towards me. She used to discipline him some- times for his smart mouth and other infractions, but I, as the younger one, never dared to talk back. I was more like her, I guess. I stayed at the house with her, instead of being out running the streets with my brother. When you're surrounded by crime, drugs, violence, and gangs, you need a rock to lean on, and despite her substance and alcohol abuse, mom was my rock.

Gang Life

Growing up in the gang-ridden streets of Little Rock, Arkansas, during my teenage years, there was no walk in the park. To provide some context, our neighborhood has even been the subject of two different HBO documentaries entitled "Banging in Little Rock." Some folks describe a gang as a tight-knit bunch of brothers, somewhat like a football team or even a family, all committed to watching each other's backs. In some ways, it might seem that way, but there's a critical distinction: gangs operate under the banner of a specific flag or color, something that can paint a target on your back instead of offering protection.

That said, being a part of a gang did provide a form of protection for my brothers and me, as unlikely as it may seem. For one thing, it expanded our circle of "brothers and cousins" since we didn't have immediate blood relatives in the city. However, it also came at a hefty price - we earned far, *far* more adversaries than allies. Nonetheless, it was comforting to have people looking out for me. I could walk down the street with a group of ten individuals instead of just my brothers and me. I consider myself fortunate to have survived those tumultuous times, navigating through a myriad of perilous situations, including drive-by shootings, violent school conflicts, and the overwhelming drug epidemic of the I 990s.

Additionally, I had to be cautious about the colors I wore and the areas of town I ventured into; a wrong choice could have meant life or death. During those years, you couldn't go *anywhere* without witnessing gang fights and shootings. Yet, with my faith and the choices I made, I not only survived but also managed to maneuver through it all.

Upon our arrival in Little Rock, it didn't take long for my brother, Aaron, to start building connections with local gang members. I often tell him he chose the path of Darth Vader instead of good old Luke Skywalker. We were both like Jedi in a sense, but he harnessed his potential for the wrong side. Over time, he rose to prominence as one of the key figures in a local gang. I knew I couldn't venture down the same treacherous path. It just wasn't my thing. Yet, as Aaron's younger brother, I found myself indirectly associated with the neighborhood gangs simply because of our relation. In this world, it's pretty straightforward: if your brother happens to be a leader in a Blood gang, you're a blood! They called me "Little DC," and there was an unwritten rule that Little DC had to follow in Big DC's footsteps. This continued until my high school years; I was like a mirror image of Aaron on the streets.

It's essential to clarify that while I was affiliated with gangs, I never dealt drugs, never inflicted harm upon anyone, and never partook in the initiation rituals known as "jumping" others. My role was primarily representing my neighborhood alongside Aaron. As I grew older, though, my involvement in the gang lifestyle deepened. By the time I was eighteen- or nineteen, I'd been banging for three to four years, and my status as a gang member was widely recognized, earning me even more clout within the organization.

In retrospect, I believe it was my instinctive decision- making that kept my younger brothers and me safe from the full consequences of the gang lifestyle. I didn't make the conscious choice to go all-in; instead, I directed my focus toward football and academics. However, to be honest, there were moments when Aaron came dangerously close to drawing me in. It wasn't a matter of him forcing me, but rather, I felt a certain pressure-I knew I *had* to conform to some degree. I didn't really have much of a choice. I knew I had to stand right alongside Aaron because if he ever needed me, I had to be there for him. If he started a fight or got into selling drugs, I would have to go down like a soldier. It was a pretty militaristic dynamic; Aaron was the General, and he needed his top soldier.

There was a time when he asked me to sell drugs for him. I responded with a resounding "No," and he essentially disowned me for it. He'd taunt me, saying, "You're such a*@#&*@ punk!" and had plenty of other less-than-flattering words to describe me. For roughly two years, he barely spoke to me, except to belittle me for not being entirely "down." I endured this because I didn't want to become a drug dealer. I had no interest in breaking the law, especially considering my mother's struggles with substance abuse during my high school years. Aaron had opted for a path leading to a lifetime of addiction and legal issues, while I made the conscious choice to pursue a more positive and constructive path.

For all my younger brothers and sisters who might not fully grasp the power they hold, here's a truth that needs to be understood: when you make the decision to step away from gang life, it doesn't follow you. You can relocate, start fresh in a new state, and evolve to a point where you can choose new friends and a different identity. That's precisely what I did. I went off to college, miles away from my former life, and eventually realized my dream of playing professionally, which became my salvation. Was I technically still affiliated with the gang? Yeah, in a way. The people who knew me were all aware of my past, but I had broken free. I like to think of it as *graduating* from gang life.

For those of you who might be toying with the idea of exploring what gang life has to offer, stop right now and reconsider. Gang members often portray it as being centered around love, brotherhood, and family, especially if you come from a broken, unloving, or even an abusive home. Sure, it can seem like a family in those circumstances, but I assure you, it's not. Instead, it leads down a dark and treacherous path, from which many do not emerge unscathed, if they emerge at all. I refused to subject myself to that kind of self-imposed adversity. Instead, I harnessed the natural challenges that life had thrown my way to develop my social awareness.

I honed my survival skills to a point where I created opportunities to succeed in different environments. I transformed into a fighter, a fighter *in* and *through* adversity. When challenges arose, I pushed back even harder, recognizing the limitations of my social environment and the complexities of my family situation, and how these factors influenced the successes and failures within such family structures. I comprehended my place within all of this. During those years, adversity became a tool that I might not have always fully grasped, but I used it to mold my determination. Each time something negative happened, I fought back hard against it. This was the way for many members of my family, but I managed to be particularly successful at it.

1st Down: The Natural

"Yet in all these things, we are more than conquerors through Him who loved us. For I am persuaded that neither death nor life, nor angels nor principalities nor powers, nor things present nor things to come, nor height nor depth, nor any other created thing, shall be able to separate us from the love of God which is in Christ Jesus our Lord." *Romans 8:31-39*

Part I - High School

In junior high, when I looked **in** the mirror, I didn't always see the kid I wanted to be. Many of the other kids had possessions I didn't fancy clothes, name-brand shoes, and designer backpacks. Even my cousins and other family members seemed to have things that were out of my reach, and as a result, I grappled with my self-steem during those formative adolescent years. Finding the right balance between academics and athletics was another struggle for me.

As I mentioned earlier, we relocated from Pine Bluff. to Little Rock. Little Rock was a **larger** city with more schools and more diversity. In this new environment, some of the coaches and teachers were black, and they invested significant time in me as a student and as a person, making me feel more at ease. Little Rock Central High School is a national monument with a rich history of civil rights activism and progress. Even then, it boasted a consistently strong football team but also had to contend with a constantly shifting, gang-riddled landscape. As a somewhat undersized tenth-grader, I knew I wasn't **likely** to make the varsity team. My confidence was far from rock-solid, and my work ethic was still a work in progress. While the coaches saw potential **leadership** qualities in me, this was still the era of old-school football, and I wasn't quite ready for it.

In my junior year, I encountered a coach who was incredibly obstinate and deliberately challenging to deal with, leading me to sit out that football season. Back then, a coach's authority was often undisputed and unchecked. For many of the players at Central, life outside of football was increasingly hectic and dangerous, as well. Doubts began to creep in, and I questioned whether my dream of becoming a professional football player was indeed just that...a dream. So, I ended up shifting my focus towards my family. I took on work responsibilities, assisting my mom in caring for my brothers and navigating her addiction.

The team's leadership didn't offer a clear path for my success on the field, so I prioritized my family over my athletic ambitions. I made a comeback during my senior year and secured the starting quarterback position. It was the first time I had received significant playing time since my 7th-grade days. In reality, I was still relatively inexperienced when it came to excelling as an athlete. If you were to read my biography and learn about my accomplishments as a football player and coach, you might assume that I was a standout high school football player. Well, I wasn't really that good at football in high school; I never received any major awards or significant recognition in any sport. Part of the reason might have been my age - I was a year younger than most of my senior peers, as I started school early. As a seventeen-year- old senior, many of my classmates were eighteen or nineteen and had an edge in maturity. I was a late bloomer, but I possessed the determination to achieve whatever I set my mind to. I had a broad skill set and just enough of everything it took to become the starting quarterback for Little Rock Central High School.

My high school experience was a bit like the historical movie, "Lean on Me." We had our very own Joe Clark, named Mr. Hickman. He was a strong, well-educated African-American principal who led with an iron fist and a compassionate heart. The harsh governance was a daily necessity due to the stark realities of our local community. The school's population had a racial split of approximately 60% white and 40% black, but the black population was generally more impoverished and from urban backgrounds. Violence felt like a daily occurrence, with metal detectors at the entrances and security officers conducting random in-class searches. It was common to see ambulances on school property because of insane high school gang fights involving dozens of students. Our environment was undeniably dangerous and volatile.

Interestingly, even with all the violence, Little Rock Central High School had a rich artistic culture and was a melting pot for academics trying to navigate the challenges of daily school life. Many of us managed to make our way into college and become productive citizens. Today, many of my former classmates have successful careers, and we frequently reminisce about our shared experiences. One thing we all agree onf is that high school life was incredibly precarious, but we're grateful we survived and have thrived in our adult lives.

The school's history stretches back to 1957 and the "Little Rock Nine", a group of nine African-American students who bravely enrolled in Little Rock Central High School during the desegregation era. Initially, these students were barred from entering the racially segregated school by the Governor of Arkansas until President Dwight D. Eisenhower's intervention permitted their attendance. The National Guard was summoned to escort the nine students through the school as hundreds of segregationists gathered outside, vehemently protesting the integration of public schools. They were a violent and angry mob, hurling profanities, racial slurs, and political biases at the "Little Rock Nine."

While a different racial climate existed in 1957, I attended Central High School in 1991, a time when the Rodney King case was making headlines. I remember clearly that when Rodney King was brutally beaten by the LAPD, the African-American students in my school organized a sit-in. The white students at our school were deeply apologetic and empathetic. This generation of Americans showed more remorse than in the past. It was evident that our nation was entering a new era, and the ability to stand together in the face of tragedy held significant meaning. Although there was still a racial divide, it had transformed into a more political issue compared to the 1950s and 1960s. Nevertheless, there were lingering memories of a race fight a few years before I entered high school, characterized as a conflict between white and black students. So, when I attended high school two or three years later, the racial divide was still present, but there was also a sense of

32

empathy. There was this half and half kind of mixture of students. One half were the gangsters who were made to go to school, and the other half were the college-bound, national merit, semi-finalist type of students.

We all had to coexist in the same space, sharing the same air, classrooms, and lunchrooms. Despite the economic and social divide, the hallways were always bursting with a sense of pride at being at Central High School-we knew about our history, and we were trying to fight to overcome it.

However, when I transitioned from ninth to tenth grade, I experienced a remarkable growth spurt. In my younger days, I was a short, chubby, athletic kid, and because of my stature and extra weight, my peers thought it necessary to try to bully me. So, fighting for respect had been a daily part of life. I was kind of a tough kid from an even tougher neighborhood, and I had learned a thing or two about protecting myself. But when I transitioned from ninth grade to tenth grade, I grew about five or six inches. I went from being five foot seven to over six feet tall in just one summer. The once-insecure, chubby kid was undergoing a profound transformation and gradually growing into his newfound confidence. I embraced my increased height, and suddenly, the attention of girls began to shift towards me. This transformation had a significant impact on my confidence, making me feel more at ease in my maturing skin. I'm not entirely sure where my height came from, given that my father was five foot six inches tall, and my mother is five foot two. Nevertheless, I felt blessed to have this height, and the added confidence it brought was certainly a perk.

My high school journey was, in many ways, typical. I balanced a part-time job, participated in sports, looked after my younger siblings, and stayed clear of trouble. I was, for the most part, an obedient child. While I did have some involvement with gangs and minor encounters with alcohol during my junior and senior years, it didn't go beyond what my mom expected of me. I was trustworthy, maintained decent grades, and became academically proficient throughout high school, which laid a strong foundation for college. I'm proud of my ability to tune out the distractions, including drugs and the presence of gangs in my neighborhood and at school, and prioritize my academics. I had positive *"distractions"*, if you can call them that - I had a girlfriend, I was into sports, and I was involved in the school band. Despite these

33

commitments, though, I managed to concentrate on my studies and performed quite well. It was a huge accomplishment for a kid growing up in challenging circumstances. Graduating from high school was another milestone because it meant I had successfully navigated and survived the environment I had grown up m.

Once I turned thirteen, my mom told me she stopped worrying about me because she saw that I was taking her lessons to heart, and our relationship was healthy and reciprocal. The same was true with my stepdad, Thom.

During that transitional phase, I was trying to discover my own identity through my faith in Christ and my passion for sports. I followed a path of positivity and sought to inspire others. My connection with God grew more intimate during my high school years. I made a full commitment to Christ when I noticed my mother was starting to succumb to her struggles with addiction. I can honestly say that I fought fiercely for her. I drove her to work, picked her up from work, took her grocery shopping, and held the keys to her jeep to ensure she wouldn't endanger herself or anyone else. Balancing all of this was definitely challenging, and I really needed strength during that period. I was searching for answers.

Thankfully, there was a local church right up the street from my house, Second Baptist of John Barrow, which I began attending. At first, I kept to myself because I was just a teenage kid going to church on my own. I'd walk, ride my bike, or get a ride from a friend or my high school sweetheart, but regardless of how I got there, the church became one of the few places where I felt genuinely safe. Becoming part of a church family played a crucial role in how my relationship with Jesus began to shape me. It was during this time that I learned to rely on Him and lean on Him for guidance in all the decisions I had to make. I would pray and surrender things to God, trusting Him to direct me on the right path. To this day, that's exactly what I still do.

It was like a light switch turned on within me during that period, filling my mind with positive thoughts such as " *You are going to be successful You won't be like your father.* From that moment, I committed to taking the steps necessary to achieve success. I believe that when someone had a father like mine, you either become a reflection of him or choose to be the exact opposite.

Throughout high school, I continued to serve God by attending church regularly and doing my best to align with His plan for my life. I didn't know then that I would become a football player, a coach, or a mentor. All I knew was that I was determined to be successful, and I paved the way for that success by becoming a jack-of-all-trades.

***

I was smart enough to secure summer internships within the engineering program at the University of Arkansas. These internships were not only a great learning experience but also kept me from spending my summers in the dangerous environment of my hometown. Although my internships were focused on engineering, during high school, my dream was to become a doctor. I believed that being a physician would allow me to blend my passion for people, my faith in God, and my desire to make a difference in people's lives. I envisioned Dr. Kahlil Carter as an amazing title, a goal I still aspire to achieve. At that time, the thought of becoming a professional athlete hadn't even crossed my mind because I didn't believe I was good enough to make it to college in sports.

But God showed me otherwise. It's fascinating how He reveals truths to us and instills changes within us to steer the course of our lives. I believe that at some point, I asked Him for this. They say that if you delight yourself in the Lord, He grants you the desires of your heart. Deep down, I think I always had a longing to be an athlete, but I never truly believed it was within my reach. Yet, when I recognized that I possessed an athletic "it -factor" and asked God for guidance, He granted me the desire of my heart. God has given me everything I've asked for, except for immense wealth, although my family makes me a very rich man. You see, I've never prayed for money. Instead, I've prayed for success, and He has fulfilled that prayer, and my blessings are abundant and bountiful.

As far as life direction goes, I value the advice of others, but I still run everything by God during our heartfelt conversations, patiently awaiting His response in whatever form it may take. My mother taught us that God may not come when you call Him, but He's always on time. Embracing this principle and promise has shaped me into a patient servant of God. While patience may not be one of my strong suits in general, I have become increasingly patient when it comes to waiting for God to reveal His answers and guidance.

I firmly believe that getting ahead of God means getting ahead of our blessings, and lagging too far behind means missing out on those very same blessings. Developing a personal relationship with God and walking in faith has allowed me to discern the true nature of the people around me and to distinguish between those who genuinely serve God and those who are self-serving. Moreover, I don't particularly resonate with individuals who are motivated solely by self-interest. God endows us with discernment because His spirit lives in you. He uses that discernment to help us understand people's intentions. While we may occasionally be deceived by smooth talkers, God reveals the true character of the people around us if we stay attuned to His voice and will for our lives.

***

I sometimes laugh when I reflect on my senior high school football team, which, quite frankly, wasn't very productive. It was the year 1994, and we finished with a one and nine record, which, to our embarrassment, was the worst in our historic school's tradition. It's worth noting that our team had two future NFLplayers and several other college-level athletes, so on paper, we should have been better than we were. However, our team faced a significant setback because eight or nine starters decided to quit right before our senior year due to conflicts with the head coach. We were essentially fielding anyone in pads, which explained our struggles on the field. The team was depleted and deflated.

Our head coach, Bernie Cox, was a throwback, as old-school as it gets: a stern, hardcore, aggressive, and a no-nonsense type of man. He had little tolerance for discipline issues or excuses of any kind. To be honest, he bordered on being not just a tough coach but also showed signs of being racially insensitive and severely tone--deaf at times. I believe that, during that time, Coach Cox held the record for the longest-tenured senior head coach in the state of Arkansas, eventually earning a spot in the Arkansas Hall of Fame. Nevertheless, he was an extremely challenging individual. I distinctly remember him once telling me in the middle of a game my senior season that I was the worst quarterback he had ever coached. His abrasive coaching style was far from inspiring or nurturing for young players.

I spent that entire year playing scared. I was still trying to grasp the fundamentals of the game, and our offense was far from innovative. Our strategy essentially boiled down to either handing the ball off or throwing it to our best receiver. Unsurprisingly, we ended up losing a lot of games with that strategy. It was one of the toughest tests of my adolescence. I was David, and Coach Cox was my Goliath; all I had was my faith and my dream. I can honestly say he almost made me hate football, but I never accepted his criticisms as fact. I was even motivated now to prove myself. I wanted to prove him wrong.

And I did.Nonetheless, I graduated high school with a bad taste in my mouth from football. I had struggled because of all the discriminatory things I had faced in junior high school at Pine Bluff. On top of this was Coach Cox, all the gang violence in Little Rock, my mom's substance abuse, and dealing with authority figures who didn't look like me and weren't invested in my success. What I didn't know at the time was that there was still a whole

road ahead of me. As I graduated, I never **looked** back. I was off to college soon, and another opportunity to reinvent myself was right around the corner.

Part II - College

I walked on to the University of Arkansas football team. You might be thinking: *With everything you had to endure in your neighborhood, at home, and at school, how in the world did you do that, Kahlil?*

This is how.

***

It was the last game of my senior year in high school, and we were facing off against Little Rock Catholic High School. It was an exceptional game for me; I ended up throwing for nearly 200 yards and running for almost a hundred. Unbeknownst to me, recruiters from the University of Arkansas were there to observe a player on Catholic's team. They couldn't help but notice my performance and reached out to me afterward. It certainly didn't hurt that my mother held the position of Director of Admissions for the University of Arkansas Medical School. As a result, I was awarded a partial scholarship for engineering that covered books and some tuition. The agreement was that I could walk onto the basketball team and play football as well. Because of my mother's absence, I had to handle much of the application process on my own, from completing all the necessary paperwork to applying to the NCAA Clearinghouse. I remained in contact with school officials, and in time, I became eligible to participate in college sports.

In the fall of 1994, I officially became a member of the Arkansas Razorback football family. It was one of the best decisions I ever made, given the school's quality and the program's reputation. While making friends had always been relatively easy for me, maintaining those relationships was often more challenging. I had a rugged exterior, but a very articulate and academic presentation. I guess that was intimidating to some, especially when it appeared that I came from an urban area but had the intellect of someone from an upper-middle-class family. What nobody knew was that I was grappling with spiritual and emotional challenges due to my upbringing and my relationship with my mother.

One cool thing was that the instructor's aides also served as my football study hall tutors. While I didn't require as much academic assistance as some other student-athletes, it was still valuable to have teachers review my work and guide me toward success. I had heard stories of students having their work completed for them, but I was a capable enough student that attending study hall wasn't mandatory for me. Nevertheless, I chose to go, given that I was a walk-on and chose not to reside in the athletic dorms. It provided me with a sense of camaraderie and made me feel like a part of the team.

The reason I chose to go to the University of Arkansas in the first place was because the state of Arkansas lacked a professional football team. In many other states, the top-rated college team essentially serves as their pro team. For instance, in Iowa, the University of Iowa and Iowa State University compete on and off the field for fan support and favor. In Arkansas, there was a solitary top dog, and we were it. The level of fan support was incredible, and the atmosphere at the games was electrifying. There was even an unwritten understanding that Arkansas wouldn't compete against in-state schools like Arkansas State, a smaller Division One school, to maintain a firm hold on recruiting. The state's allegiance to Arkansas was unwavering, and it was the obvious choice for me coming out of Central High School. From the moment I set foot on campus, all I heard was, "Woo Pig Sooiee!" This spirited chant permeated the very atmosphere of the campus, and aside from the sports programs, the university boasted one of the nation's top engineering schools. It felt like home to me. I appreciated the fact that the University of Arkansas was far enough from Little Rock. I believed that this distance would provide me with the best opportunity to escape the neighborhood and succeed academically.

My freshman year there was marked by numerous unique experiences. Academically, I changed my major from pre-med to psychology when my mother battled depression and began to confront her own demons. I struggled to comprehend how a straight-A student and diligent single mother, who was like a wonder woman, could be so deeply affected by depression. It was an Introduction to Psychology class that shed light on her condition. The class delved into the study of behavior and mental processes, exploring how we think and act. I realized that everything in life hinges on these two aspects: what happens to us and how we react to it. This class exposed me to some serious truths. Some of my questions were answered, and the more I learned, the more I developed a strong passion for wanting to help people understand themselves, others, and society. But psychology wasn't the only thing on my mind... my other "major" was football.

This was another crucial period of athletic development for me, though I did not develop athletically as much as I should have; I was tall but still thin. Transitioning from a neighborhood marred by gang violence, low school attendance, and a failing football program to competing at a highest level, and at the state's premier football program was a defining moment in my journey... both academically and athletically. I joined as a walk-on in the same class that produced NFL players such as Brandon Burlsworth,

Anthony Lucas, and Madre Hill. We all immediately stood out in our fall camps.

As walk-ons, Brandon and I posed challenges for our defense every day, while scholarship players like Anthony and Madre had the privilege of practicing with the varsity. On the scout team, we would dress up as the opposing team and run their plays. With the talent Brandon and I had shown, we managed to achieve success against the defense during that first season. Excelling on the field created friction with the upperclassmen because a walk-on should never outshine a scholarship player. We defied that daily, and during my freshman year and throughout my time there, I was seen as an adversary.

You'd think that playing better than some of the players on scholarship would be good for competition, but I quickly learned that wasn't true. Instead, it made the coaches look bad. It made the players look bad, too. Being a talented walk-on who exuded confidence and had his own set of friends created a divide.

While some coaches appreciated my determination and passion, others seemed to despise me for it. My background and financial situation set me apart, and some coaches dismissed me year after year.

However, these challenges only fueled my determination to become a better player, dispelling the negative opinion of my high school coach. I remember one game during my freshman year when we were facing Vanderbilt at home. I had a great week of practice simulating Vanderbilt's quarterback. With our team comfortably ahead, they actually considered putting me in the game. But then Head Coach Danny Ford stopped me and said, "No, no, no, he's redshirting." I wasn't the least bit upset; in fact, I had a huge smile on my face. It was a sign that I was making a positive impression on the coaches during practice, and I was just thrilled to be considered for playing time. I truly believe that great coaches know how to develop a young player's skills and prepare them, and I was fortunate to have good leaders in the locker room. I had come a long way from the timid quarterback at Little Rock Central High School to a versatile athlete at the University of Arkansas, and I was making a name for myself on the team, both positively and negatively. A metamorphosis had taken place: I had made a huge jump from the scared quarterback of Little Rock Central High School to a versatile athlete at the University of Arkansas.

My journey at the University of Arkansas was one of constantly adapting to a prestigious sports program that seemed larger than life. I was a *preferred walk-on,* meaning I was recruited but not offered a scholarship. Additionally, I was also one of the only, if not the only, player from Little Rock schools on the team at that time. The University of Arkansas hadn't been recruiting students from Little Rock due to the plague of gang violence in the city, but I saw it as an opportunity to demonstrate that Little Rock schools still had respectable talent and class.

My arrival at U of A made me feel like a baby guppy in a Koi Pond. Because of my walk-on status, my confidence, and my bravado, some of my teammates went out of their way to show their displeasure with my presence. Even now, all these years later, some of those same guys are not friendly with me because of my pro career that resulted from playing at U of A. I could practically hear their thoughts: *"How could this walk-on make 1t further than me?" "No way can this walk-on be better than me!" "How in the world can this walk-on have such a confident mentality?"*

As my former teammate Donnell Fletcher said, "I don't think the word 'no' is in Kahlil's vocabulary, and the word 'can't' is most definitely not in his vocabulary. That's something he doesn't even speak of, so if somebody would try to use that against him, that right there would drive him more than anything else to prove the person wrong. That kind of drive certainly drove the more complacent teammates away. But Kahlil didn't care."

I believe my background, upbringing, and the influence of my mother played a significant role in how I viewed and carried myself. Coming from the East Coast and living in Arkansas, my speech, walk, and style of dress set me apart. As Donnell Fletcher noted, "Kahlil was kind of an East Coast type of guy. He'd wear polo sweats and Timberlands, and being from DC, he had the East Coast kind of swag, but he still represented Little Rock."

Culturally, I was much different than many of my peers, which sometimes made me feel like I was perceived as "weird" or "strange" by others. However, I embraced my individuality because I enjoyed marching to the beat of my own drum. I fit in certain ways, but in others, I didn't, and I was perfectly fine with that.

The University of Arkansas football program was everything I ever dreamed of, with all the bells and whistles I could have hoped for in a program. Wearing Razorback red and being a part of such a prestigious program was the greatest opportunity I had experienced up to that point in my life. Looking back, I'm incredibly thankful that I made the decision to attend U of A, and I owe much of it to my mother for paving the way for me.

I felt like I was performing on the football field, and the coaching staff was talking about me every day. I felt like I was part of something larger than myself. Helping the team prepare each week for SEC-level opponents made me feel like I had an important role, and I relished that. When we played Tennessee, I was Peyton Manning. When they needed a dynamic returner or running back, that player was me. Whatever role they needed on offense, I was ready to fill it. Interestingly, I initially joined as a quarterback but evolved into a receiver and a returner. Between these three positions, having the football in my hands made me a dangerous player. Many players recognized my contributions, including stars like All-SEC running back Madre Hill and All-SEC wide receiver Anthony Lucas. They both told me I had what it takes to play at that level, which filled me with confidence. Madre was arguably one of the best freshmen running backs in the SEC, and Lucas left a legacy at Arkansas as one of the best in school history. Competing against All-SEC level players in practice, many of whom went on to the NFL, further reinforced my confidence. I knew where I wanted to go and what I wanted to accomplish...! just didn't know exactly how I was going to get there. That *how* was up to God.

During that time, God surrounded me with many influential people, one of whom was Brandon Burlsworth, my walk- on teammate. Brandon and I developed a close friendship. We were both ambitious and stood out on the field. We engaged in numerous conversations about our futures, sharing meals, and

spending time together during those first couple of years. However, when the movie "Greater: The Brandon Burlsworth Story" was released, I was not mentioned, and our relationship was left out of the story. I imagine they wanted to include the more well-known players, but Brandon would be a huge motivation in my professional career.

Rest in peace, Brandon. You inspired me more than you realize, and my entire professional career was a tribute to your life and the fragility of life in general. Thank you.

***

During the Spring of 1995, I had proven that I belonged on the team, at least athletically. I was being recognized as a player on the rise. I received compliments from many of my scholarship peers who believed I had what it took to play in the SEC and, according to Anthony Lucas...even win the Heisman Trophy one day. In practice, I honed my skills by emulating dynamic players from opposing teams, such as Peyton Manning, Danny Wuerfel,

Fred Taylor, Jacquez Green, Peerless Price, and any other offensive threat from opposing teams. I was celebrated by coaches for being a nuisance to our top-rated defense and given credit for helping them prepare each week. I was starting to benefit from all of the collegiate coaching and competition, but it was short-lived as the program never intended to honor their commitment to me regarding earning a scholarship.

I later realized that I may have come across as too well to do for a walk-on. My mother was an important administrator in the University of Arkansas school system, and I was indeed from a different side of the tracks than many other recruits. It would take me three years to truly understand this, and in the meantime, I made the most of every opportunity to improve.

During Spring Drills, I was surprisingly elevated to the second-team quarterback while our true starter played baseball and the other Quarterbacks either transferred or graduated. I excelled that spring and grew significantly as a player. I dedicated all my time to the weight room and film room, often neglecting my studies as a result. Newspapers were buzzing with my name, and my family couldn't have been prouder. However, something stood out during that time: my mother's absence. She was consumed by her own struggles, and I felt very alone. No one was ensuring that I studied, got adequate rest, or stayed accountable. As a result, I failed academically, even though the coursework wasn't too difficult. The assignments just didn't compare to the joy I derived from playing football. This was a significant departure from my usual academic focus, a prerequisite to play sports in my home. Without my mother's guidance, I lost sight of my priorities and what had got me there in the first place.

Spring 1995 passed, and I took my chances of earning a spot on the team along with it. In retrospect, it was my own fault; you see, I knew how to succeed. I'd forgotten how easy it was to fail.

***

The fall of I 996 brought a series of challenges that were beginning to weigh heavily on me. Not only was I dealing with my mother's full-blown substance abuse, but I also knew that my brothers were involved in gang and drug activities. To add to the complexity of my life, I had become a new father. I felt like I was fighting against the world, grappling with the diverse dilemmas that stereotypically derail African Americans and learning from each one.

These circumstances, coupled with the expectations of attending a large university, made it extremely difficult to balance everything *and* focus academically. Looking back, I realized that I had failed myself by not putting in the same amount of effort that got me into the University of Arkansas in the first place. I believed I had it all together and thought I was smart enough to pass classes, but I didn't give my best effort.

The result of all this internal and external pressure was academic suspension. I was back home in what I considered "Gangland USA." This suspension also put me in bad standing with the football team. My position coach, Fitzgerald Hill, and head coach, Danny Ford, were supposed to help me, but they didn't. I was just one grade short of being eligible. I had seen more being done for players who didn't even try academically. It was frustrating because, as a good kid from a dangerous urban environment with a strong academic history and good test scores, I felt like I was being abandoned and sent back into such a perilous environment.

I shared how the University of Arkansas coaching staff and support system had let me down during my academic suspension. It was a challenging time for me, and I felt like they missed an opportunity to make a difference in my life, preserve a talent, and help protect me from my difficult environment. Their lack of support was disappointing, but I remained determined to find my way back to school, no matter the obstacles in my path.

The year away from playing football at the University of Arkansas was a very pivotal time in my playing career. There were a lot of distractions, socioeconomic perils, and life changes happening. I became a new father at age 18. My environment was drastically changing. My mom's addiction was weighing heavy on me. My priority to my new family became my number one priority. Graduating from college was still a goal, as was returning to play for the razorbacks. I had very little contact with my position coach, namely Coach Fitzgerald. I never understood the disconnect between him and I, but as he later would tell me, "Sometimes student-athletes fall through the cracks." Still, I worked various jobs to take care of my mom and her transition, and took extra classes to regain my eligibility. I learned that it was gonna take a concerted effort on my part alone to get myself back into good standing with the team and live up to my full potential. I grew a lot during this time, and I realized that failure was not an option.

**

As part of my plan to return to school, I made the decision to completely separate myself from my gang friends. Although they had protected me and were like family, I knew that their path would lead to danger and trouble. Many of them would face tragic fates such as death, addiction, and incarceration in the coming years. Despite the emotional connection, I had to follow my own path and trust in God.

When I finally returned to the University of Arkansas after my suspension, God willed that I'd be fortunate enough to encounter a remarkable educator named Dr. Kilambi, who taught biology. Unlike my coaches, he had a different approach to teaching and wouldn't allow me to fail. Recognizing my intellect and dedication, he noticed my consistent efforts in class, sitting in the front row, and submitting assignments on time. Dr. Kilambi acknowledged my determination and regularly invited me to his office to ensure I fully grasped the material. Despite his thick Indian accent, which many found challenging to understand, I appreciated his wit, demeanor, and intellectual prowess.

Dr. Kilambi wholeheartedly embraced my return to college by challenging me academically. During my initial college experience, I had become caught up in the hype of Division One football, resulting in academic struggles and missing two entire seasons. This time, I was determined to reach my full potential, graduate, and become the best version of myself, even if it meant putting football second. Consequently, I was relegated to the scout team, but I continued to work diligently and improve with each passing semester.

The journey became even more challenging when I witnessed my former walk-on classmate, Brandon Burlsworth, flourishing as a great player on the varsity team. I desperately wanted a chance to prove myself as well, so I pushed myself harder every day. Just as Spring ball approached and I began to turn heads, my worst nightmare came true-I suffered a stress fracture during drills. This injury prevented me from participating in spring practice, and another fracture during rehabilitation kept me out of summer camp as well. I had come so close to becoming the next walk-on to earn a scholarship, but these foot injuries set me back significantly.

I felt disheartened because this was an opportunity for the coaches to provide guidance or tell me if I had a chance at all, but they didn't invest the time in me. Despite all the obstacles I had overcome and the sacrifices I had made to be part of the team, they seemed indifferent. It made me seriously consider transferring. If I could challenge our SEC defense in practice, surely there would be another place where I could make a meaningful contribution.

As soon as I could catch my breath with school and football, I noticed that my mother and brother were struggling in Washington DC. I needed to convince my mom to check into rehab and find her way back to God. My younger brother was getting involved with the wrong crowd, selling and experimenting with drugs at only fifteen years old, so I felt as though I had to rescue him. I had always been his protector and father figure. I made up my mind to create a home for him, even though I was still a young man myself. Taking the biggest and scariest step of my life, at age 20, I decided to marry my daughter's mother, transfer away from my beloved University of Arkansas, put my mom in a spiritually based rehab, and move my brother in with me and my new wife. I didn't know what else to do. People needed me to be a man, so I became one! I had no idea what it was going to take, but I knew God would carry me.

I married Elizabeth in the spring of 1997. Most of my friends didn't get married until they were well into their thirties, while I was already married at age twenty. My friends couldn't understand it and couldn't believe I had made such a big commitment at such a young age. Elizabeth reminded me of my mother...short in stature but big in heart. As a co-captain in high school, Elizabeth was also my biggest cheerleader. She had helped me through a difficult time during my mother's substance abuse in my high school years. She had firsthand experience of what my family was all about. In fact, she was my family. She filled my adolescence with mostly positivity instead of the negativity that came with gangs, drugs, and violence. At the same time, she was dealing with her own volatile home situation. When we met, she found someone with ambition and a vision to escape a bad home environment-someone with a love for God. I found someone to inspire and share my ambitions with, and I could clearly see that she had that fire inside of her, waiting to be brought out. I believe that much of what she is doing now in her life is based on our time together. It took both of us growing and maturing to become who we are today.

After the fall semester of 1997, Elizabeth and I left our home in Fayetteville and returned to Little Rock to be closer to her family. At that same time, I made the decision to transfer to Southern Arkansas University as a junior in the spring of 1998 to continue chasing "the dream". Looking back, transferring to Southern Arkansas University was probably the biggest mistake I made in my young football career. Thankfully, I gained a year of eligibility back and continued to strive academically, but the environment in that small, rural, southern town made me regret my decision to move there. As a black man in the South, I felt very unsafe and unimportant.

That fall, my brother Randi came to live with me in Magnolia since our mom was going into rehab. Randii attended the local high school there, and now as a 2I-year-old, I became his guardian. I had to care for him as he was my son instead of my younger brother. I would wake him up in the morning, make his breakfast, lunch, and ensure he got to school every day. I still had to attend my own classes, go to football practice, quickly come home to check on him and make sure he was doing his homework, and then focus on my own course work. Despite these responsibilities, I managed to make the Dean's list for the third straight semester. However, I was now fulfilling roles as a new husband, father to a toddler, full-time student-athlete, and guardian of a budding young adult. I was doing all of this on my own, without any financial assistance from anyone in my family.

During that time, I heavily relied on God by staying in prayer and reading the Bible. I needed His help on the field, in the classroom, and in my marriage. It often felt overwhelming, but God granted me the strength and endurance I needed during that period.

Part III - Pro Life
Arkansas Twisters

Professional football had always been a dream of mine, but it seemed almost impossible after my college experiences. However, everything changed when an arena football team came to town in the spring of 2000. As I was wrapping up my degree at my third university, after giving up my final year of eligibility, I decided to give pro football a shot. I had dominated intramural sports over the past few semesters. My first workout for the Arkansas Twisters was in January of 2000, although it felt more like I was helping the others try out rather than trying out myself.

Following my initial workout, the coaching staff continued to bring me back to throw to the talent they were evaluating. Through this experience, I was able to showcase my skills and gain traction with the staff. The time came to sign contracts, and I found myself on the outside looking in. Some of my close friends, who had played at the University of Arkansas., were getting signed.

I prayed for just an invitation to training camp, but that's when God showed up and intervened. During one of the final signings, I was invited inside the office, where Head Coach John Jenkins said to me, "Kahlil, you did an incredible job for us, and we want to give you a chance to come to training camp and compete for a job."

My immediate thought was... *What? No way!*

Here I was, the "Rudy" of the team, getting an opportunity to showcase my talent. After all, I had only played one year of college football, not even as a quarterback, and it was at a division II school.

I'll let John tell it in his own words: "When I worked Kahlil out, he looked like a player who was inexperienced, yet I could see he had some talent, some ability. But he wasn't an exceptionally God-gifted player like some others I had seen. He was a very gracious, polite young man. I could tell by my initial meeting with Kahlil that he was a very fine upstanding young man because he was very attentive. He was full of yes-sirs and no-sirs.

"At the end of that practice, I had the players who tried out complete an information form, and I told them, 'Fellows, I will be in touch with you. If I have a genuine interest, we'll take it to step two.' So, after that first tryout, I would rate Kahlil as basically very borderline. And even though he was young and very rough fundamentally, he had this overwhelming sense of confidence about him. I did not sign him immediately. However, when I staged the second tryout camp, he was one of the first ones to show up, and immediately, I noticed his desire and perseverance to try out for another position. And, you know, Kahlil, from the neck up, is as brilliant as any player I've ever seen in my forty-something years coaching pro football and major college football."

Coach Jenkins saw something in me. When I asked him about it later, he shared:

"I learned years ago from a legendary coach who's now passed away: 'You better watch out for guys who possess a lot of God-given ability and yet they don't really enjoy practicing. And furthermore, if they get comfortable with a lot of money in their pockets yet don't really have a great love for the game, you'd better hang on because they're 'fixin' to shut it down on you, and you will not be able to depend on these guys regardless of their ability, regardless of their talent. I will never forget that. Kahlil was not one of those guys."

Despite facing discrimination during my time at the University of Arkansas, I felt as though my dream of becoming in the NFL was all but dead. However, in a surprising turn of events, a man offered me an opportunity that I will never forget. He didn't know anything about my background, yet he believed in me and provided me with a chance. This opportunity eventually led to me earning the MVP title at training camp. I couldn't help but think, *Finally, all that burning tenadty and determination inside me has paid ofif* I pushed myself beyond my limits, giving my all, and ended up becoming the backup quarterback for the team.

Now, let me tell you this: no matter how skilled you are, the backup quarterback doesn't get much playing time. However, it is crucial to be prepared in case the starting quarterback gets injured. The Arkansas Twisters completely changed my perspective on what I could achieve. I went from a long shot, to training camp MVP, to the first player in team history to sign a pro contract with the AFL. After that successful first year, each subsequent year became an opportunity for me to improve and excel. My teammates and friends would often tell me, "Kahlil, you were just lucky, while some admitted that I outworked everyone. While they were partying and having fun, I was in the gym, doing drills, lifting weights, and attending tryouts." See, I didn't consider that luck; I saw it as destiny!

Coach Jenkins once told me that I was one of the most dynamic and versatile players he had ever coached. Hearing those words from him meant a lot because he had coached numerous great players, including all-time greats in the USFL and NFL, like Jim Kelly and Herschel Walker. It was truly an honor for me. During that first year, I didn't get much playing time, but whenever I did, I was able to compete at a high level against former Division I athletes, some of whom had spent time in the NFL The first year of the Arena Two League was extremely competitive, and despite our team's underachievement, it provided me with the opportunity to develop, compete, and showcase my skills. That year became the launching pad for my successful professional career, but it also presented me with a lot of decisions to make. Should I return to the Twisters or try my luck at the next level? The team wanted me to come back as the starter the following year, but I wasn't sure if that would happen. While Coach Jenkins admired my skill set, I wasn't fully convinced that he believed I could perform as the starting quarterback, and perhaps I had doubts about myself. So, I went to the league office and obtained footage of all the games I had played in. Back then, we used VHS tapes, so I connected two VHS recorders to create a highlight tape of my biggest plays from my first season. I still have those VHS tapes to this day. I sent that highlight reel to every losing team in the Arena Football League, hoping that a coach who hadn't won many games might see my potential and give me an opportunity. And then it happened.

Milwaukee Mustangs

The Milwaukee Mustangs had a rough season the previous year. I signed a contract with them in 2001 because of my connection to Coach Jenkins, who was the Offensive Coordinator a few years earlier. The Mustangs played their games at the Bradley Center. Coach Rick Frazier, the head coach, was someone who genuinely cared about me as a player and treated me like a son. Our relationship grew strong during my time on the team. He pushed me hard, was very critical, and coached me to the extreme. Despite being a backup quarterback, wide receiver, and defensive back, I played in every game as a rookie. Surprisingly, I was nominated for the All-Rookie T earn in 200 I as the team's representative. According to Gary Compton, one of my older teammates, "Kahlil was a kid that would compete each and every day." And I did.

After that season, unfortunately, the Mustangs had to cease operations because the Arena Football League was unstable at that time. Some teams were able to afford their stadiums and salary caps, but others, like the Mustangs, had worn out their welcome at the Bradley Center. The team just couldn't solve the scheduling conflicts that prevailed with the Milwaukee Bucks, which contributed to the team's departure.

Toronto Phantoms

After the Mustangs folded, Coach Frazier became the defensive coordinator for another Arena Football team, the Toronto Phantoms. The Phantoms were the only AFL team located in Canada, and I was the only player Coach Frazier drafted from the Mustangs to accompany him there. In a dispersal draft, players from a folded team became draft able by other teams to select Coach Frazier continued as my mentor, and our relationship grew even stronger. He introduced me to Mark Stoute, who continues to be a mentor for me. Both Coach Frazier and Mark Stoute taught me how to *real.play* the game. They took me from being a novice at multiple positions, including quarterback, and turned me into a ball-hawking defensive back. I played in about nine games but gained valuable experience, guarding the best receiver in the game every day in practice.

There is no question that Damian Harrell sharpened my skills as a defender. Damian is easily one of the best players in Arena Football history, both statistically and athletically. Disappointingly, even though the Phantoms were a strong team, we underperformed, but the growth I achieved that season was detrimental for what was about to come. I will forever be grateful for that experience.

Tampa Bay Storm

At the end of that year, the Phantoms also ceased operations. My journey through professional football had just begun, but it had already been filled with twists and turns. I went from one league to another and from one team to another, even within the same league. It sometimes felt like a yo-yo, with constant ups and downs. When the Phantoms folded, I was drafted in yet another displacement draft by the Tampa Bay Storm, a team coached by the legendary Tim Markham. Markham was known for his incredible success in arena football. I attended training camp with high hopes, but unfortunately, I didn't make the final cut. Tampa Bay went on to win the championship that year, thanks to their stacked roster of talented players. Being cut from the team was a tough blow for me. It was my first experience of failure in this profession, and it was hard to accept that they didn't see my potential. I knew I could have made a valuable contribution to their already impressive lineup. But that's just the nature of football. Almost everyone gets cut at some point.

Arkansas Twisters to the 2nd Power

After being cut for the first time and not being picked up, on waivers, I returned home to my AF2 (arenafootball2) team, the Arkansas Twisters. After all, that's where my family was-and that's where the team that had given me my first big break. However, being back home didn't bring me happiness. My marriage was falling apart, my career felt like it was in decline, and I was experiencing a spiritual struggle.

I began playing with a chip on my shoulder. I was intent on being the best player ever. I no longer possessed the likable and humble demeanor that had made everyone want to root for me. I decided to rely solely on myself and took my chances. I started working out like crazy and doing everything necessary to achieve success. That season, I won player of the year and broke the professional football record for interceptions in a single season. My speed on the field was unmatched-I could effortlessly run 40 yards in 4.3 seconds. At 6'1" and 185 pounds, I was a lean, mean running machine. All in all, I accomplished some amazing things on the field without regard for the sacrifices that it cost me personally.

Buffalo Bills

My exceptional performance during the season caught the attention of NFL scouts, and I was being flown all over the United Sates to try out for teams. The Cleveland Browns were the first to recognize my potential. Coaches Butch Davis and Chuck Pagano personally worked me out and offered me a contract. I spent weeks in Cleveland without ever touching the field as I was released right after signing a contract so they could sign a Quarterback who became available. Not long after, one of the top defenses in the NFL came calling. I worked out with the Buffalo Bills in the middle of my player Defensive MVP season, and in February of 2004, they signed me. Interestingly, I was already in training camp with the Orlando Predators under the guidance of Coach Jay Gruden. However, Coach Gruden allowed me to pursue the opportunity.- in Buffalo, and I eagerly accepted it. It was a dream come true, and I was determined to make the most of it. I intensified my training even further, which unfortunately led to the development of a sports hernia. It was a huge setback, but I refused to let anything stop me, not even an injury.

NFL Europe

After joining the Buffalo Bills, I was allocated to play in NFL Europe in 2004, where I had the privilege of being coached by the legendary Jack Bicknell. Coach Bicknell had gained fame as the head coach at Boston College during Doug Flutie's time at Boston College. He was also well-known for coaching numerous All-Americans with NFL potential in NFL Europe. Having Coach Bicknell as my coach was an exciting opportunity, and I was eager to play under his guidance. See, being an African American from an urban environment, living and playing in Europe opened my eyes to the endless possibilities that existed in the world. It was a transformative experience to be able to visit and witness other cultures and historical sites that I had previously only read about. This exposure had a positive impact on me.

My time in Europe was a valuable learning experience, and our team traveled all over the continent. As a member of the Scottish Claymores, we toured the beautiful Scottish countryside, from Glasgow to Edinburgh. We learned about the inspiring story of William Wallace, and the Scottish fans embraced us as if we were one of their own. Living in Scotland was one of the most gratifying experiences I had ever had as a football player.

During our twelve-week stay, we played ten games and as one of the team leaders, I had the opportunity to further develop my leadership skills in the secondary. I played a key role in implementing a system that allowed us to effectively communicate and translate calls, signals, and colors, ensuring that our exceptional defense was always on the same page.

Having recently won the Defensive Player of the Year award in the AF2 league, it felt like the world was mine for the taking. My plan seemed to be working, but I questioned whether God was pleased with the way I was living my life. I would soon learn that the greatest lesson as a player was not about success, but rather about humility. It was a lesson I needed to be taught repeatedly. Unfortunately, the injury bug struck again, derailing my unorthodox journey, and this time, I genuinely knew my NFL dream was over.

See, during my training for the NFL, I made the decision to participate in a non-profit flag football game against the local police and fire department. It was a cold and miserable day in

November, and unfortunately, I strained my groin while giving my all to win that game. In hindsight, it was not a wise decision to even be out there, considering I had a private workout scheduled with the Cleveland Browns. It was a risky move on my part from the beginning. The groin strain followed me to Cleveland and then to Orlando and even to the NFL Europe training camp, eventually developing into a sports hernia. I was putting my body through intense lifting and running without proper rest, icing, or treatment. The pain was excruciating, and I couldn't believe this was happening. Despite the agony, I didn't miss a single game or practice; instead, I chose to conceal my injury.

During my time in NFL Europe, I had the privilege of being under the medical supervision of Dr. Brian Andrews, a renowned sports physician for the NFL. However, he misdiagnosed me with an inflammation of the pubic bone instead of a sports hernia. It was during the early years of these pseudo- hernias, and diagnosing it accurately was challenging back then. It wasn't until I had a workout with former Philadelphia Eagles legend, Keith Jackson that I realized something was seriously wrong with me. Keith advised me to see his trainer, and upon doing so, she immediately stretched me out and said, "Yeah, something's wrong."

I wasted no time in calling my old head trainer at Arkansas, Dean Weber. Dean always treated me with kindness and respect. He forwarded me to one of the leading doctors in the area and made me an appointment with a surgeon, who correctly diagnosed me with a sports hernia. How could Doctor Andrews have missed this? Did Buffalo even want me? Navigating through the doubt and the injury was incredibly tough, and I didn't know what Buffalo would do. Despite our exceptional season in Europe (which boasted one of the best defenses in the league's history), I returned to the United States still injured.

Back to Buffalo

I wasn't sure if Buffalo had a vested interest in my recovery, and I found myself unsure of what steps to take. I was filled with fear, worrying that they would release me for being injured. Despite this, I reported to camp still feeling the effects of the hernia. Inevitably, Buffalo ended up releasing me, even with the injury. At that moment, I had to figure out my next move. My mind was flooded with thoughts, racing like a running back on Combine day.

Should I file a grievance against the Bills for releasing me while still injured? What should I do about my injury? Would I ever be able to play football again? Indecision and fear consumed me, so I turned to prayer. I sought support from my prayer partners, as well as my mom's prayer partners, who laid their hands on me and fervently prayed for my recovery.

Ultimately, I decided not to file a grievance against the Buffalo Bills, even though it meant forfeiting a portion of my contract. So, I settled for just the reimbursement for my medical expenses with the expectation that Buffalo would make good on their promise to bring me back when healthy. Other teams continued to express interest in signing me, but my experiences made me wary of joining a new team without a signing bonus or protection. I was a six-figure earner in other leagues, and I had given up my insurance and retirement to pursue my dream. If I could be easily released without the protection of the union, I didn't see risking my health as a viable option. The NFLPA seemed to almost dissuade me from filing a grievance. In the end, I chose to return to the AFL. The league that I trusted.

Toronto Argonauts and Nashville Kats

In 2005, I found myself back in the realm of arena football. While I was in Europe, my rights had been traded from Orlando, and I was signed to a two-year deal by an NFL-owned team. At that time, I was still in the early stages of healing from my hernia surgery, and the team leveraged that to sign me for cheap. I felt a strong desire to prove myself and make my way back to Buffalo. Joining the team in Nashville was particularly appealing because it was close to home, allowing me to focus on my struggling marriage and make a case to the Tennessee Titans, who owned my new team.

The season started off slowly for me as I was only three- or four-weeks post hernia surgery. Initially, I was overlooked for rookies, but once I was given the opportunity to step onto the field, I became one of the most dominant players in the league. I finished the season with an impressive seventy tackles and seven interceptions in only 13 games. I believed that such a performance would surely catch the attention of the Bills or even the Titans. After all, I had come back from a hernia surgery.

Buffalo never called; The Titans never showed interest. Even my agent backed out on me, leaving me on my own, once again.

That year, the Nashville Kats boasted the number one defense, and I was grateful to be recognized as Second-Team All- Arena at both corner and safety positions. However, my ultimate goal was to win a championship. While I was proud of my season, there was still a lingering sense of emptiness. My thoughts were consumed by the NFL daily, and despite my hard work and accomplishments, there seemed to be little to no interest from the Bills or the NFL as a whole.

Returning home once more, I decided to take on a job at an alternative high school, where I could serve as a mentor for at- risk youth. The principal of the school was Charles Jones, a distinguished individual who was not only a fraternity brother but also a former Razorback football player. He believed in me and hired me to be a role model and administrator at the alternative school. I felt deeply that this was my calling. as I had a natural ability to inspire young people and help them realize their dreams.

Then, one random day in 2005, while I was at work, I received a call from the Toronto Argonauts, a CFL team, expressing their interest in having me play for them. I was uncertain about what to do. On one hand, I was fulfilling a meaningful role in my community and had the support of my friend, who believed in me. On the other hand, an opportunity to continue playing football had presented itself. When I shared the news with my fraternity brother, he simply smiled and encouraged me to go for it; fully onboard with the opportunity, and understood the depth of my dream. With his blessings, I made the decision to pursue the opportunity.

During my first season with the Argonauts, I didn't see much playing time. I only participated in the last game, which allowed me to re-sign with the franchise for the following year, in 2006.

Playing in both the Arena Football League and the Canadian Football League was a demanding but highly rewarding experience. I was fortunate enough to be one of the last players to compete in both leagues while being under contract with the other openly. After my brief time in Toronto, I returned to Nashville in 2006 with two contracts in hand: one for the AFL and one for the CFL.

In Nashville, I was honored to be selected as a pre-season All-AFL player. Arena football had treated me well, and I wasn't quite ready to give it up. However, there were some concerns about the direction of our team. Despite having a dominant defense, the previous year, new off-season acquisitions left me uncertain about our future. As the season progressed, we encountered a series of messy games and experienced a significant amount of discord within the team.

Frustrated with the situation, I requested a trade away from the Kats; I was ready to go win a championship with another team.

Orlando Predators

The Orlando Predators were renowned as one of the top franchises in AFL history, led by the exceptional coach and Hall of Fame arena football player, Jay Gruden. Jay and I maintained a close relationship even after my short stint in 2004. Early in 2006, I was traded back to Orlando due to my dissatisfaction with the intense environment in Nashville. The team had lost its competitive edge, and there was an abundance of complacent behavior among the players, and it affected the team.

When I joined Orlando, the team had also played below expectations, like Nashville, and needed a missing piece to become a championship contender. I was that missing piece. With me added to the lineup, we would go 7-3 for the remainder of the year. Our success was attributed to a dominant pass rush and excellent QB play. I would say I had one of my best games ever on national television game when I was with Orlando. This game re-instilled the confidence that had guided me throughout my career and prepared me for the upcoming CFL season.

Although we made it all the way to Arena Bowl 20, our defense was lacking key components. Nonetheless, I had played some of the best football of my career up to that point. Even though we fell short in the championship game, I was ready for the big field!

Toronto Argonauts Part 2

After the Arena Football season in 2006, I made my way to Canada and joined the Toronto Argonauts. I had the opportunity to play in 13 games with them, including the eastern divisional championship. In total, I participated in nearly thirty- five games throughout that year. I dedicated myself wholeheartedly to the

2006 season, giving everything; I was spent mentally, physically, and emotionally. Despite that, I now had a place to call home in Toronto. However, I couldn't foresee Father Time slowly catching up with me.

During my time with the Argonauts, I had the privilege of meeting Damon Allen, a CFL Hall of Farner. Damon had already been playing for almost twenty years when I joined the team. Although he was an offensive player and I played on defense, we quickly formed a strong bond. Damon once mentioned, "During my time in the CFL, I played on multiple teams, and I understood the importance of having a good relationship with my teammates, because we're all trying to put our team in a situation where we can win championships. Most of my friends were on the defensive side of the ball, and I was an offensive player, and that has a lot to do with the fact that I spent so much time dissecting defenses."

When asked about my defensive abilities, Damon commented, "Kahlil had a talent for getting his hands on the ball and he had the capacity for making big plays as a defensive back. Kahlil was a good teammate, one of the leaders on the team, and we formed a solid friendship." I gained a deep admiration for Damon because he was already established in the league as one of the all-time greats. Damon Allen always said that I had (FBI) or Football Intelligence but really needed to learn how to fit the puzzle. "As a player, I listened to Kahlil talk about his skillset and being the *peoples champ.* And he was really, really good, and although it was great for him to have that kind of confidence in himself and his skillset, at times, his attitude was perceived to be arrogant, or that he thought he was bigger than the team. I think, in some respects, it probably rubbed some players the wrong way, but the reality of it was that Kahlil's personality had the ability to clash with other teammates because they perceived it to be selfishness. I didn't find Kahlil to be a selfish player at all. He was just sure of what he could do on the field, and he wasn't timid about telling you. I always liked his confidence, but I was quieter about shouting it out in a public setting. You either loved Kahlil or you hated him-there was no middle ground."

Damon's message to me was always this: 'I've learned that even the people who don't like you, there's a message you can probably learn about why they don't like you. You can find something about yourself that you may have to correct, even from the guy who doesn't like you, and you can also learn from someone who does. The ones who don't like you may have some complaints, but, you know, there are lessons woven within all those complaints, so use them to self-evaluate because sometimes it's the people who are telling you the truth that might be the truth about yourself you haven't faced yet.

"Whether you're a player or a coach, the fundamentals are the same: every time you step on the field is a day to get better. How do you get better as a coach? How do you get better as a player? How do you communicate better? All these things are life lessons you must learn when you start getting into leadership and coaching."

NFL, CFL, versus AFL

The desire to play in the NFL still burned within me, but the few teams that reached out were offering only training camp invites. I already had contracts that included bonuses and insurance for my family, so I just wasn't willing to jeopardize those guarantees for a chance as a third or fourth-string backup. I made the decision to stay where I was. My NFL dream died in 2006. I was 30 years old.

I had become a highly sought-after free agent in the Arena Football League, and I was also earning a significant income by playing in the Canadian Football League. The truth is, I didn't want to give up being a star player in two leagues just to become a role player in the biggest NFL. I was tired of being a long shot, even though the financial rewards would have been much greater. I just wanted to play! I didn't want to be on the sidelines or caught up in the politics of football. That's when I reached out to my former defensive back coach in Nashville, Brenard Wilson.

Brenard had been my coach in 2005 and 2006, and he had previously been a defensive back for the Philadelphia Eagles during their Super Bowl run in the 1980s. If I were to describe Brenard as a person and coach in just two words, they would be humble and exceptional. I called him and asked, "Coach Wilson, I have an opportunity to return to the NFL. T earns are contacting me. Should I go?"

He responded calmly and straightforwardly. "Kahlil, you have to decide between jumping through all these league hoops and chasing your dream. Do you want to be the star or the backup? Because that's what it comes down to."

"I want the money!" I replied.

Brenard immediately shot back, "Money is something you should consider, but money never lasts. What lasts is the experience. Do you want to play, or do you want to watch?"

"I want to play," I finally said.

Brenard then offered me advice that would stay with me. "Then you might want to stay in the league that already respects your game."

And so, I stayed.

My football career continued to thrive, although I occasionally reflected on whether or not I should've kept pushing. I wrestled with these thoughts without the guidance of an agent, father, uncle, or any other real support. However, in the end, I asked God to guide me. Could I keep putting football above everything?

By 2007, I began to realize that my career was reaching its end. After finishing the 2006 season with the Toronto Argonauts at the age of thirty, I accomplished many of my goals: Making it to the NFL, and still dominating at a highly competitive level in professional football.

The only issue with Toronto was that I just didn't have the full confidence of our defensive coordinator, Rich Stubler. He was old school. Things like me swimming in the end zone after an interception wasn't his favorite thing to see. I just wish he would've stepped up to establish clear standards for our team. As a result, we never became the team of destiny that I hoped for. See, a winning team requires the right combination of individuals who work together harmoniously. Rich always emphasized, "It's not about the twelve best, but the best twelve." I didn't understand it as well then, but I have embraced this philosophy and applied it in my own coaching career-you need the right mix of guys to make magic happen on the field. He called it F.I.F.O. From (2005-2007), we played in three divisional championships with the number one defense in the league, and I was there to contribute to our team's victory, but Coach Stubler was more than a coach. To many of the guys on that team, he was like a Guru. Toronto helped shape my character, my future and my future coaching career.

From the beginning of 2007, I regularly rotated between the AFL and the CFL. My AFL contract had been following me around since I left the NFL, taking me from Orlando to Indiana, and ultimately to Kansas City. Returning to Arena Football marked the beginning of the end for me in Toronto. Toronto was furious at my choice to play in 2 leagues, but I was able to take advantage of a rule called "the "First Contract" and make double the money. The league fought against it. Now, in order to switch leagues, players must get an exemption from their league or be released. I don't regret my decision, but it undoubtedly played a role in my demise in Toronto.

I returned to Toronto in 2008 with a separated shoulder from playing in the AFL and Rich Stubler, now had become the head coach. Let's just say he was no longer a fan of mine. I had to face this reality repeatedly during the final training camp. Although I performed well in camp, the toll of all the football I played was catching up with me. I had grown tired of being treated as a backup, experiencing defeat at the finish line, and witnessing favoritism. I was not one of Stubler's guys anymore.

Frustrated with these circumstances, I demanded a trade or release like I did two years earlier in Nashville. I prayed about it and decided to try my luck again. The last time ended at the championship. It was a risky move, especially at the age of 31, and as a result, I decided to play in a playoff game in the Arena Football League with my favorite coach, Jay Gruden, and Orlando on 3 days' notice. My friend needed a favor, and the coach needed a veteran play maker. I was a mercenary at this point. A veteran who could play in any system and excel. I didn't know where my future would take me, but God had the wheel. One week after the game, Montreal from the CFL reached out to me to play in one of their games. Being a veteran of both leagues, plugging in and playing wasn't a major challenge for me. Football was football, and I had accumulated extensive experience at a high level over the years. It made perfect sense for me to join Toronto's rival team in the Eastern division, as it gave me an opportunity to seek a little padded payback for the way things ended there. However, the transition wasn't easy, and I had to prove myself with a whole new team and former rival.

The Montreal team, now under the leadership of Marc T rest man as their head coach, brought in a new era marked by discipline and a no-nonsense approach. Initially, I experienced my first real adversity as a veteran, but an opportunity presented itself, and from om that point onwards, I never looked back. I played throughout the playoffs and earned a starting position in my first Grey Cup appearance. T restman, at the end of the season, shared a sobering reality with me: "As much as we love the game of football, it does not love you back." I understood what he meant. Yes, I had bounced around from team to team and league to league, pursuing my dream, but I was also mentored by so many great coaches. I felt like I had accomplished enough. I had achieved everything I wanted in football. It became clear to me that the writing was on the wall. I was 32 years old, grappling with neck and back pain, carrying the label of a journeyman player, a 3-year- old torn labrum in my hip, and without any championships to my name. It felt like the end, especially in the CFL; this is where my journey should end.

***

Every coach I had the privilege of playing for was an influential figure in my life. Coach Jenkins, with his illustrious history in college football and experience coaching in so many leagues. He gave me my first opportunity in pro football. I'm forever grateful. Rick Frazier, one of the pioneers of specialized defenses in Arena Football, was known as a great man to work and play for. Also, there was Gary Anderson, a former All-Pro NFL running back and an exceptional black man to play for. Being under Gary's guidance showed me firsthand what black excellence looked like, and I learned a great deal from witnessing his humility both on and off the field. Coach Anderson was one of the most down- to-earth individuals I've ever met, and he truly appreciated my abilities.

When asked about my work ethic, Gary said, "Kahlil owned the field when we had drills. He wanted to be the first one in line. He wanted to be a leader and show what to do and how to do it the right way. I guess he was preparing himself to be a coach like he is now. To be a good coach, you always must be a good leader."

He continued, "On the field, Kahlil didn't take foolishness. Sometimes, it was kind of hard for him to relax because he was always in that serious mode. He was there to do the job, and any athletes reading this, as a player, when you hit the field, that's how you've got to be...you must come in to play ball, not to play around. Kahlil had that X-factor from day one. He's got that up-beat, almost high-strung personality. He's always excited and ready to go, ready to make things happen. One thing I remember is that Kahlil liked to play gags and jokes on everybody else, but he didn't like it when you pulled jokes on him. Just an intense, fiery personality."

Another notable figure in my football journey was Pinball Clemons in Toronto. He was renowned for his charismatic efforts in the community and his humble nature as an African-American man who valued faith, family, and excellence. I also can't overlook the impact of Jay Gruden. Playing for a legendary former player was a tremendous honor. Tim Markham, Jack Bicknell, and John Gregory are other coaches whose names are synonymous with exceptional coaching and exemplary (FBI) in the football world.

It was because of them that I transitioned into coaching with immediate success. I owe my growth as a coach, both personally and professionally, to the invaluable knowledge I gained from these exceptional men. Their mentorship provided me with a distinct advantage, and I utilized that knowledge to continue my personal and coaching development.

As a coach and businessman, I was beginning to see success by leveraging my status as a former athlete, although I realized that I had approached things in the wrong order. I put football above everything, but unfortunately, my relationships with my loved ones and with God suffered as a result. Some people may have viewed me as cocky or overly confident, but those qualities were precisely what made me a great player. I always had a chip on my shoulder...ever since high school.

I remember during my time in high school, a classmate of mine bestowed the nickname "Kahlil 'The Real Deal'" upon me, and it had nothing to do with football or sports. He said, "You're like this really cool dude, a genuine person... I can tell you're the real deal. I guess I had forgotten that. When I was younger, I was a gladiator. I was a Claymore...! was William Wallace. Now, I was seeing the finish line, and it bothered me. When asked about my competitive nature, Donnell Fletcher remarked, "Kahlil has fire inside him that gets stoked when someone tells him he can't do something or doubts him. His self-belief is amazing. And honestly, that self-assuredness can sometimes rub people the wrong way because some may interpret it as arrogance, but it's simply him having faith in himself." I was cool with that because playing football requires a bit of madness. You need to have confidence in yourself to excel in that game." I have that streak of craziness, confidence, and cockiness because I genuinely believed that no weapon against me shall prosper and that I was more than a conqueror. With God by my side, I experienced various social conditions within the African-American community and emerged stronger. After everything I had been through, I had every reason to believe in myself.

Everyone who knows me will undoubtedly say, "Kahlil comes across as cocky," but I simply believe in proclaiming myself as the best. Muhammed Ali serves as an iconic example of confidently stating that he was the greatest, undeterred and unaffected by those who heckled him for what seemed like an inflated ego. Another one whom I idolized growing up is Deion Sanders. His confidence is his greatest superpower. People often say that you don't need to tell others how good you are; they should be the ones to recognize and acknowledge your greatness. I partially agree with this sentiment. However, I also believe in proclaiming the gifts I received from God and living in my purpose. We don't talk about who the greatest Canadian Football League player of all time is because that player isn't wealthy or famous. Unfortunately, if you **didn't** make your career **in** one of the major **leagues**, people don't even see you as a professional athlete.

2nd Down: The Notebook

"And let us not grow weary while doing good,

for in due season we shall reap if we do not

lose heart."

Galatians 6:9

Retirement

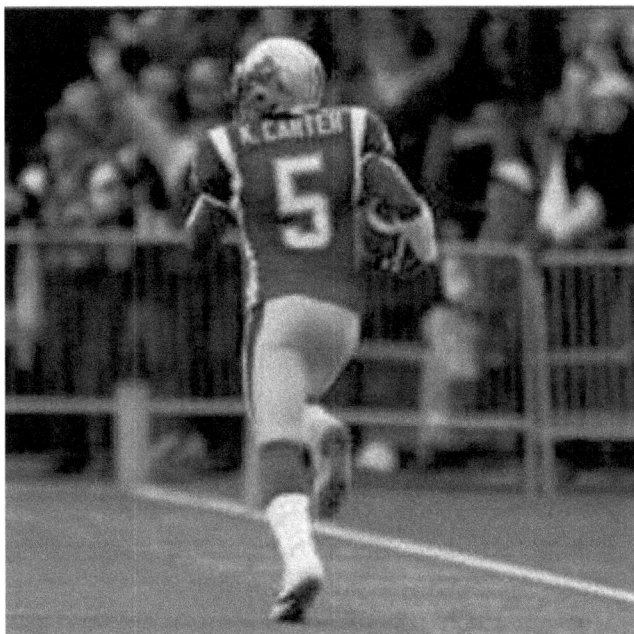

My 2010 season would be my most physically challenging season to date. I was in the best shape of my life at the beginning of the season, but during this season, my body began to wear down a lot more than I thought. Whereas it would take me 1 or 2 days to recover from a game, now it would take me 3 to 4 days to recover, which made me miss the majority of the week to practice. But since I was a player-coach, I did more instructing on those days than simply performing. By Thursday or Friday before the game, I would practice and acclimate myself to the game plan, and this was not my normal process. I began to see my skills diminish, and I was missing more plays than I ever missed in my career. I was learning other valuable skills relating to coaching and administration for the team. This presented some challenges for my teammates, who had never seen a player also be the coach. Coach John Gregory mentored me on some of the finer aspects of being a diplomatic leader in order to resolve some of the conflicts.

I finished the season with average stats for me, and by the end, I felt like I had accomplished everything I needed to accomplish as a player. My dreams of the NFL were now long gone, and my career in the CFL had been exhausted. Now, it was time for me to focus on a new journey of transitioning into a professional coach, something that my majority of coaches have always said I would be successful at. I can remember my last game as a player. I was struggling physically to keep up with some of the younger players. There was a game in Arizona against the famed Arizona Rattlers. They were play-offs bound, and a victory by us would extinguish their home-field advantage hopes.

I loved playing spoiler, and even though I did not have my best game, we won as a team, and I was proud of the growth the team had shown during the season. We would finish with the third scoring defense, the number one against the run. I walked away from the game, completely satisfied with all the accomplishments I had achieved during my career, so it was an easy decision to retire at the age of 33. Other teams would send me contracts in subsequent years, but I knew that my best years were behind me. Retiring on my own terms felt like the right decision for me and my family. I wasn't sure if 1 would miss the game, but I was hoping that coaching would give me the same validation as playing, and I was right.

The prospect of coaching professional football was just as exhilarating as scoring touchdowns and making interceptions. Not many players have control of their destiny in this way, but I was one of the lucky ones. From a walk-on to a long-shot to a backup to an all-star - what better way to retire from the sport that I love? The six-year-old living in me was proud. Mission accomplished. Dream fulfilled.

The best part of retirement was that I met my wife, Courtney Marie, a dreamy, green-eyed beauty with an extremely friendly and nurturing disposition. She enjoyed sports as much as I did, as she had played sports her whole life growing up but wasn't a die-hard fan. From the moment we met, we had a mutual passion for each other. Me, ending one journey as a retiring athlete and her beginning hers as a budding young mother. We had so much in common and related so well, even though we were from different parts of the social spectrum. Courtney was the woman I needed to become my best self. She would be that supportive influence as I began the pursuit of giving back to the game I loved through coaching. Ask any married coach: Having a supportive "coach's wife" is essential to the process of doing the job. My wife epitomized this person. She patiently waited for me to finish grad school, she lovingly allowed me to pursue opportunities in Canada, and she was a real partner as I went off to different start-up leagues year after year. All while taking my lumps in the profession and eventually figuring out how to be the professional I evolved into. She was an awesome good luck charm. I had my best games while she was in attendance in my final year of playing. We were undefeated at home in Calgary over my 3 years and 20+ games there, and although we would lose back-to- back championships, my wife was right there with me in below-freezing temperatures with two little kids... cheering louder than anyone in the stadium. See, I have 4 daughters in total. God's cruel gift and curse for men wired like me. I mean... no sons to carry on the torch? Thanks, Lord. My oldest two daughters from my first marriage, Briana and Brooklyn, never really forgave me for divorcing their mother. I broke their hearts, and there would be nothing I could do to ever heal them or myself. Kids are always the ones who suffer the most when parents can't work out their relationships. My kids became collateral damage in a war I didn't even need to fight. I now know that God wants me to be a man after his own heart... a father. .. a husband... a servant. .. a believer. To live in God's purpose for my life, taking care of my family has to be the priority. God blesses me for being a faithful steward over my family and that includes my adult children and even my ailing mother. For too long, I put football at the same level as my family and probably my faith.

Retirement would allow me time to reconcile, and mend broken bridges... or so I thought. Finding a balance between family and coaching would bring its own challenges, but none that I would have to face alone. My wife would be the foundation for it all. Happy wife, happy life is true.

Part V - Amateur Coaching
The Beginning

In 2007, I found myself back in Arkansas, and Coach Gregory was still in charge. It was during this time that he offered me my first paid coaching position. I was ecstatic! This was not a volunteer role, but rather a paid opportunity to do what I loved. I was appointed as the Pass Game and Special T earns Coordinator. One of the defensive backs I coached during my first year was Tanner Varner, who later became my teammate. According to Varner, "It was nice having a defensive coordinator right alongside you. He would say, 'We know they're going to run this play next. This is what we need to do.' It was great having Kahlil as a coach because he taught me a lot about strategies, and it was also great having him play alongside me."

Tanner once commented on my communication style, stating, "Communication with Coach Carter could go either way it depended on whether you could handle the way he talked to you. Some guys could, some couldn't. His communication style never bothered me. He's very opinionated and confident in what he says.

If you disagree with him, he will stand his ground, and that can sometimes land him in trouble."

I coached for the Twisters for eight games from March to June before attending training camp with Toronto. I distinctly remember that during that time, we had a record of six wins and two losses, putting us in first place in the league. Ultimately, the team finished with an outstanding record of twelve wins and four losses, having a remarkable season. Three of the players I coached received all-league recognition that year. It dawned on me that I had the ability to do this - to coach. Although I didn't complete an entire season with the team, the players embraced my coaching, teaching, and leadership. They carried on with the same dedication and passion even after I left. They even asked me to coach them in a playoff game, though we unfortunately lost. Yet, seeing their growth from the beginning to the end confirmed my belief that I had a future in coaching.

It's worth mentioning that success in the CFL, AFL, and NFL can look different. The NFL has a win-at-all-costs mentality, and job security tends to be limited. On the other hand, the CFL and AFL share similarities with the NFL, just on a smaller scale. In the AFL, if a coach is doing the right things, being productive, and winning some games, things are generally considered good. In the CFL, every team, except for three, makes it to the playoffs. This means that regardless of how poorly a team performs, if they don't finish in the bottom three, they still have a chance to compete for a championship. The stakes might not be as high as the NFL, but the pressure is still there.

As a CFL coach, particularly when I worked with a Coordinator above me, I experienced immense pressure. The CFL is a highly competitive league, and the level of pro football is exceptionally high. Winning requires extensive preparation, logistics, creativity, innovation, and humility. However, there are also moments of disappointment and then a lot of picking yourself up off the ground. I had a lot of success in the CFL; we had a great record, winning around fifty out of sixty games. Unfortunately, we lost two championships, which was a significant blow. Those two championship losses plummeted back to ground zero. I mean, landed hard, real hard, especially after the second loss, which came when we had the game in our hands. The experience affected me deeply. It made me question my coaching career and whether I needed to branch out and establish my own culture of winning. I realized the sacrifices my family had made for my coaching pursuits, and I needed to reassess if that could happen in Calgary.

Through all the victories and defeats, I learned to focus on counting the costs and measuring the distance before I leap back into coaching. With that said, I must address the costs of coaching in any league. In pro football coaching on any level, there are so many graveyards of broken marriages, broken families, and fatherless kids due to the prioritization of coaching above all else. The reality is that coaching can take a toll on one's mental and physical health. It can lead to issues like alcoholism, womanizing, drug addiction, long working hours, and immense stress. Without the right support systems, coaching can be a precarious career path. At this point, I am taking a timeout to evaluate how coaching fits into my life. I have come to understand that football can never be the top priority. Personally, my faith always comes first, followed by my family. If the opportunity arises, then football comes third.

Faith. Family. Football.

Part VI - The Transition

In 2009, I was out of pro football. Fresh off a dominant playoff run and a championship game appearance in the Grey Cup with Montreal in 2008. I unfortunately found myself on the old guy's list. That same year the AFL had ceased operations, and the new United Football League was only taking regional ex-NFL players. I trained my tail off to stay ready just in case a CFL team needed me to plug in and play like I had become accustomed to doing. No teams called. No teams wanted a 32-year-old six-figure journey-man, but I continued to train like a Rocky movie. I was relentless. How dare they tell me I was getting old. I knew several 32-year-old players who were still producing, and I was one of them. The waiting game was not unfamiliar to me, but when the season came and went, I had chased long enough, and I realized I had accom-plished all I could in the CFL, so coming back to the USA to be closer to my kids was something I couldn't pass on. My children were in Arkansas, and they strongly wanted me to return home. I couldn't go back to Arkansas. Arkansas was just not a place where a progressive African-American man could be himself and elevate his status. Very few Head coaches in Arkansas are African- American. The Universities seemed to ignore black candidates, so I sought a more forward-thinking environment. And that's when God showed up again. I received a call from my mentor, the legendary John Gregory. He offered me an avenue into coaching by coming to Iowa, of all places, and joining his team as a player/ coach.John gave me my first coaching opportunity in 2007, and we experienced a great deal of success together. Plus, John promised to continue to mentor me in the profession and be a reference for jobs I was applying for as an up-and-coming coach. John was in the Iowa Sports Hall of Fame, and his connections in the state immediately paid off for me. It was another example of one of my mentors coming through for me and my career. John was a championship level Head coach in the CFL and the AFL. He had coached great players like Kurt Warner, Kent Austin, Danny Kanell, and Aaron Garcia. I trusted Coach Gregory like a father figure. He gave me a lot of great tools to use in coaching. He would always say, "Kahlil keep your knees bent...staying flexible. You always must be able to adapt and pivot." I spent as much time as I could around those coaches and was soaking up as much time as possible with them, eager to learn from their expertise. It was a relief to know that my playing days were over, and I no longer had to worry about attending training camps or engaging in putting myself through rigorous off-seasons, especially at the ripe age of 34. Instead, my focus shifted entirely toward becoming the best coach I could be. I can't overstate the significant role that Coach Gregory played in shaping my coaching philosophy. He taught me valuable lessons about team preparation, organization, and the importance of managing the variables within a team. I knew that once I left that 20 IO team, I was ready to be successful, but the hard part was just beginning.

John wasted little time making a call for me after the 20 I 0 season. In my first year, I served as a restricted earnings coach at Graceland University later that fall. Although we weren't a good football team, I was able to mentor young players who would later follow in my footsteps as a professional. My next opportunity was at Valley High School in 20II, where we would finish 13-0, capturing a State Championship. That was my first championship, and the Head coach, Gary Swenson, quickly became one of my favorite people on the planet. A reserved and humble man who was a great motivator and leader. He is who l wanted to emulate as a coach. To this day, Gary is an important part of my coaching story and its success. After the championship at Valley, Coach Swenson recommended me to Chris Creighton at Drake University. l was fortunate enough to be hired as a member of Drake University's staff as a restricted earnings coach in the summer of 2012. This meant that l was earning about $8,000 per year, which was not much at all. However, l knew that this was a necessary step in the coaching profession - to start at a low-paying job and work your way up. During those two years, I had to cover the costs for two years of grad school, but it was well worth it. In *2014*, I proudly received my master's degree in public administration 2015 would be a breakthrough year for my coaching career. I was signed to the 2014 Grey Cup champions, the Calgary Stampeders after having just been a guest coach the summer before with the 2013 champions Saskatchewan Roughriders. Coach Gregory had once again delivered on his promise to help my career. He had been in contact with both teams, leading to both opportunities in the CFL. Aside from coach Gregory's influence, I received an excellent recommendation from Saskatchewan's Head Coach Corey Chamblin, who had been with Calgary a few years earlier. Coach Chamblin saw my intellect ad ability to relate information to players. On top of all that, my good friend and former teammate Devone Claybrooks was the defensive line coach for Calgary. He was assured to soon be the Defensive Coordinator the following year in *2016*, so he wanted to duplicate the success we had when we were teammates. We shared a player-friendly, technique-centric approach to football, and Calgary was the most well-respected organization in the Canadian Football League. Claybrooks and l would go on to coach in three divisional championships and two CFL championships **in** just three years. Despite this success, I left the team to pursue my own path. It wasn't necessarily a mistake to leave Calgary, but rather a deep sense of personal disappointment and a desire to redeem myself outside of the team's leadership. I wanted to feel like I mattered to winning and to the growth of the players I was coaching. I was doing a lot of great work in Calgary, but no one knew what I was doing. I wanted to step away from that team and branch out on my own to prove that I was instrumental in our success.

I made the bold move to join the worst team in the league because I wanted to make improvements and demonstrate the effectiveness of my schemes and philosophy. I wanted to attract players by showcasing my relatable coaching style, my ability to bring discipline and technical expertise, and my knack for elevating players' performance and helping them succeed financially. When recruiting, I would emphasize my capability to enhance their skills and their earning potential. These are my strengths, not empty boasts. Thus, stepping down from a championship-level organization to join the weakest team in the league required a huge leap of faith. One of the first things I saw when I joined Montreal was that our head coach was coaching in another league during the off-season, which resulted in a lack of full-time leadership. Preparation is the key that propels one coach over another, and when a coach isn't present or dedicated, he cannot adequately prepare his team to be successful. I can't change an absentee coach; neither can I play for my players, or steal the signals, or go out there and punch the other coach in the face. What I *can* do is out-prepare him and be ready for whatever he throws at me when he *is* there.

My primary focus was crystal clear: I wanted to win a championship, especially since I had experienced three consecutive losses in the playoffs and the championship. To achieve this, I devised a comprehensive championship plan to guide this struggling team to the top. However, most of the other coaches did not share my vision. Their main concern seemed to be job security, whereas I have always prioritized performing to the best of my abilities rather than fretting about keeping my position. I understood that my performance would determine whether the team would retain me, promote me, or dismiss me. As the team adjusted to the coaching change, the new head coach took aim at his new Defensive Coordinator. Mike Sherman and I were as different as night and day. We both sought to transform the organization from the inside out and from top to bottom, but our styles clashed, and that set the stage for my departure from Montreal.

Stepping down from Montreal was a very difficult decision, but there was a lot of pressure from the General manager and Coach Sherman. They wanted to demote me for being so assertive with the staff. They also wanted me to go along with every decision that they made as it relates to personnel. I felt like I was the Defensive Coordinator in title only, so I fought back against that notion. I helped them build a great team both in free agency and through managing the Canadian ratio. But I was getting undermined by others on the staff. Rich Stubler was hired to be my Senior Advisor on defense. He was not happy in that role after coaching me as a player and also when I worked under him in Calgary. He would have private conversations with Coach Sherman about my ability to lead and win. Stuber once told Sherman, "Montreal won't win a game with Kahlil as Defensive Coordinator." Once I heard this, I stopped fighting. It was obvious that they wanted me out of my position, so I towed the company line and assumed responsibility by stepping away from the team. I realized that the media scrutiny would be intense, but stepping away also allowed me to contribute to the team's success in a different capacity, as I was not willing to accept defeat gracefully or silently. I refused to channel all my energy into organizational changes. In pro sports, my limitation lies in not being a corporate- minded individual. I am an X's and O's guy- I excel at strategizing and getting players to perform at a high level, win games, and reach championships. What I lack expertise in is organizing pay structures for managers and administrative assistants, despite having a degree that suggests otherwise. The truth is, *football* is where my focus and passion lie.

In the end, I made the decision to step down from coaching and transition into a scouting role. Becoming a scout grants me more flexibility in my schedule, the opportunity to work from home while prioritizing my family and allows me to utilize my education in addition to my charisma and talent. It was also important to me to not let anyone undervalue my worth. I noticed that in Canada, various media outlets, administrators, coaches, and even fans continuously devalued my efforts, my position, my presence, and my philosophy on the values that define who I am. Some individuals receive preferential treatment, while others are treated unfairly. I still can't understand why I received unfair treatment when I consistently played and coached with great results. I held my own against numerous Hall of Famers and overcame personal challenges to achieve success. It was disheartening to see that my success story and resilience were not respected. The people in power treated me as if I was insignificant, like a puppy crawling on all fours. That is not who I am or what I stand for. Despite being part of some of the best teams in the league and achieving significant milestones, even my own players did not fully embrace my coaching approach with respect and professionalism.

As an African-American coach, I couldn't help but question if I was hired as a token minority. This realization prompted me to do some research, and I discovered that none of the minority coaches in my position had ever been promoted. I needed to lead and pave a path for my profession that was not obstructed by prejudice and discrimination. As a player, I played my best football for minority coaches because I believed they truly cared about me as a person and not just a player. My immediate boss in Calgary, who was black, fully understood my passion, discipline, and go-getter mentality. Black Coaches face intense scrutiny, and very few of them ever make it to higher positions such as the Team President, General Manager, or Director of Football Operations. These are the positions that hold the most influence over a team and what happens with that team than the coaches. I felt like I could do this as well as I had coached the game itself. Maybe I could get into personnel, using my skills in player evaluation and team structure. I expressed my aspiration to become a general manager to Kavis Reed, the GM **in** Montreal, who, having once been a coach himself, understood my intentions and offered me the scouting role, envisioning my potential for a greater role. However, while in Montreal, I realized that they didn't want a charismatic leader; they just wanted someone to hold the title until Sherman got his guys in. The final and most important reason I agreed to walk away from Montreal was to be more present for my family and to diversify my career path, with family taking precedence. That was worth giving up the best opportunity I had to date. My family is the best thing to happen to me ever.

All the reasons I just mentioned led me to step down. Embarrassingly, I knew I was not going to be respected as a Coordinator. This made me reconsider my position. It was embarrassing to face the media, my peers, and the players I had recruited. I also had to explain to my wife and her family why my dream job had turned into a nightmare. It took me about a month to overcome the initial sting and embarrassment. After that, I got to work scouting for potential players. I offered Montreal several players. The team stumbled out to a 0-9 start, and the GM called me weekly.

Although Montreal was losing, I felt like my decision to step down was ultimately the right one. I didn't want to be considered a psychic for leaving before they suffered the losing streak, but I knew the disfunction I saw would cost them games. Calgary did things with a family-oriented, winning attitude. Montreal was a chaotic environment run by unqualified people. I would have preferred to help them win, but I chose instead not to be a part of them losing. There will always be people who whisper that I "abandoned" the team. Others will say they fired me. Still others will say, "He can't win the big game." The naysayers will always have something to say, but I knew that I had worth when Montreal approached me the next year and offered me my job back. I didn't see a change in attitude, and after watching the previous season, I chose not to work for a man like Mike Sherman. They were all fired a few months later before the start of training camp. I thought that would vindicate me, but the damage was done. I just prayed that my next opportunity would take me somewhere where I can be a part of something special, whether it's back in the CFL with one of my former colleagues who knows my coaching style, in the collegiate level where I can make a difference, or perhaps inspiring young people in the community to strive for something greater than themselves. But come what may, I know I will approach it with purpose and passion because that's what it means to live an *1Nspirationallife.*

Part VII - You're in the Big Leagues Now!

As I mentioned in Chapter 5, **John** Gregory offered me my first coaching **job** and encouraged me to come to Iowa. At first, I was skeptical about Iowa, thinking it was a place known for growing potatoes. However, Coach Gregory assured me that those crops were in Idaho, and he convinced me to join him in Iowa for a year of playing and the opportunity to pursue coaching. With that, I packed my bags and left Canada. Iowa had weathered the challenges of the depression and the recession, and its economy had remained robust. Before I knew it, I found myself **in** Iowa, ready to dive into work.

According to Coach **John** Gregory, "It was very apparent to me that Kahlil was one of the most brilliant young coaches I had ever encountered. He excelled in his ability to make adjustments, quickly identify when changes were **needed,** and evaluate areas that required improvement in the heat of battle."

Although people would often refer to me as brilliant when it came to coaching, I never placed too much importance on just words. Actions matter so much more. How do you treat me as an equal member of the staff? My ultimate ambition was always focused on winning championships and achieving greatness. There will always be individuals who are content with just being on the team, but I recognized that their complacency would hinder our chances of winning championships. Part of my style of coaching is to get the players going. Every pre-game, I would get in the middle of the huddle and come up with elaborate celebrations to boost morale. Whatever it took, from clapping everyone's hands, challenging quarterbacks, kickers, or even the offensive linemen. I was a rah-rah kind of guy, and I had always been that way, even during my time as a volunteer coach at Valley High School. It was my job to pump up the team. Coach Swenson remembers those moments, saying, "My memory of Kahlil is watching him do his pregame hype ritual because nobody else on our staff could have pulled it off and made it real. You know, the kids really bought into it and loved it. .. it created an atmosphere that I thought made it special for the players."

Whenever our team faced a challenging game and felt exhausted, defeated, or lacked faith in our ability to win, I would gather them in the huddle and pour into their very souls. Witnessing my players rise up in response to my words, and energy solidified my belief that coaching was my true calling.

3rd Down: The Network

"You are the salt of the earth; but if the salt loses its flavor, how shall it be seasoned? It is then good for nothing but to be thrown out and trampled underfoot by men. You are the light of the world. A city that is set on a hill cannot be hidden. Nor do they light a lamp and put it under a basket, but on a lampstand, and it gives light to all who are in the house. Let your light so shine before men, that they may see your good works and glorify your Father in heaven."

Matthew 5:13-16

Part VIII- How to Find a Job (Post-Sports Career)

It's no secret that many football players face uncertainty once their playing days are over. Those who have been wise with their substantial salaries are financially secure. Those who have taken steps towards securing job stability in post-playing careers, such as broadcasting, coaching, investing, or real estate, find themselves **in** a good position. However, a significant majority of transitioning or retired athletes fall into the next category: they have no idea what their next move will be. They may not have earned a substantial amount of money or may have spent a significant portion, or perhaps all, of their earnings without making any plans for their future.

Ironically, throughout an athlete's playing career, teams offer a lot of support, such as financial and investment counseling. They provide opportunities to get involved with non-profit organizations and corporate entities to give players a glimpse into life after football. They also bring back former players and coaches who share both success stories and cautionary tales about life after the game. Unfortunately, many young athletes believe they will play forever, that the next contract is just around the corner, or that their big payday is only one season away. Consequently, they fail to adequately prepare for the realities of their future. Some of these individuals have never worked a day in their lives. They have been involved in football programs or processes from middle school through college, receiving support to excel on the field. After college, they transition straight into professional sports, which may not always offer substantial financial rewards.

I can personally attest to the challenges faced when starting at the lowest level of professional football. When I first began playing at the pro level, I earned a mere two hundred dollars per game for a fourteen-game season, with a bonus of a mere fifty dollars if we won. We had to cover our own housing expenses, and we received meal vouchers to sustain ourselves during the season. I worked at Kroger's and a psychiatric rehabilitation center for children to make ends meet. Even with these jobs, I barely managed to cover my expenses. I vividly recall eating countless hamburgers from McDonald's and Wendy's because that's all I could afford, even with the meal vouchers. Through personal experience, I learned the value of a dollar, and that mindset helped me save a significant portion of my earnings, as I looked toward future opportunities rather than squandering my money based on a sense of entitlement to the next opportunity.

Getting That First Coaching Gig

When athletes transition into a coaching career after playing football, they often find themselves in one of three categories. However, it's important to note that this opportunity is not guaranteed for everyone, unless they are considered a Hall of Farner. Hall of Famers have more opportunities available to them than regular contributors to a football team. For example, players like Kurt Warner and Brett Favre were likely offered coaching jobs, and it's safe to assume that Tom Brady will receive offers as well. These individuals have established themselves as pillars of football success. On the other hand, there are many stories like mine. I played at lower levels and achieved great success, but I didn't have the same financial stability as the iconic figures in the sport.

Coaching provided me with a great avenue to continue my involvement in the game I love. Throughout my football career, I was often referred to as a "coach on the field" due to my ability to understand and analyze plays, as well as execute them effectively at the right time. Coaches and mentors frequently told me that I had the potential to be a great coach, and I believed them. With this encouragement, I pursued a coaching career. However, to my surprise, despite having ten years of professional football experience, numerous accolades, and championship appearances, I struggled to find a job. I was repeatedly told that I needed to earn my way and pay my dues. It was frustrating to see other individuals with less experience and shorter careers in the NFL being given coaching positions simply because they attended major Division I universities or played longer than I did. Since it was challenging for me to secure paid coaching jobs, I decided to take on volunteer opportunities wherever I could find them. My first volunteer coaching position was in the Arena Football League under the guidance of John Gregory. John learned to manage grow in the profession by controlling only those variables he could control. It's a lesson that also took me years to work through.

After that, I landed a gig as a volunteer assistant coach, which eventually led to another volunteering opportunity at Graceland University, a small college in Iowa. This was the same school attended by Caitlyn Jenner and the Green Power Ranger. Prior to this, I had been a volunteer assistant coach at Diggins High School in Iowa and then took on a part-time restricted earnings position at Drake University. From *2007* to 2013, I dedicated five years to voluntary assistant coaching positions. During two of those seasons, we even won championships, but I still didn't receive a promotion. I was responsible for recruiting players, coaching individuals with less athletic ability, and working within the constraints of low-budget schools and leagues that didn't offer much compensation. In my first coaching job, I made around five hundred dollars per game, and I coached eight games. Throughout my first five years, my annual income never exceeded $8,000. Despite this, I was coaching at Division I, double A college level, and handling recruiting duties. It was challenging to see a bright future, but I was assured that this was the path to success, so I persevered. I had mentors who continually praised my efforts, telling me I was doing everything right and that I was excelling in my field. I attended coaching clinics every year, often spending a significant amount of money on travel and clinic fees, although sometimes the team would cover these expenses. Towards the end of 2013, as I was completing my master's degree, I seriously considered giving up on coaching.

However, shortly before my graduation in 2014, I was offered another volunteer coaching opportunity with the Saskatchewan Roughriders, the current defending champions of the Canadian Football League. The coaching staff at the Roughriders had researched my background and recognized that I was a rising star who had paid my dues. It was reassuring to know that my hard work was being acknowledged, but once again, the position did not generate any income. At that time, I was taking my final class, accounting, and I had to miss the first two weeks to fulfill my coaching commitment in Saskatchewan. I knew I couldn't afford to miss any more class time as it would result in being dropped from the course. However, those two weeks turned out to be enough to turn the volunteering opportunity into a paid position the following year. And so, here I am, in my sixth year of coaching, finally receiving a salary that reflects my experience, education, and effort level.

I'm sharing my personal journey with you because the question for this chapter is, *How Do You Find a Job (post-sports)?* I boil it down to what I call the three A's:-

I.   Associations

2.   Attitude

3.   Appearance

Believe me when I say that having these three qualities will help you earn jobs.

Let me explain why.

Associations

We've all heard that it's not about *what* you know, but about *who* you know. I would add to that and say it's also about *who knows you.*

I remember a particular incident when I asked one of my mentors, who happened to be an African-American coach, if he could make a call on my behalf. To my surprise, he replied, "I can't." He went on to explain, "I could make the calls for you, but they won't listen to me. You need a coach of a different ethnicity to vouch for you. It's important to have some Caucasian coaches on your side because if you only associate with black coaches, you'll limit yourself to opportunities within that circle." He continued, "Kahlil, you need to network with coaches who are different from you in order to expand your connections, so that when they speak on your behalf, their words carry more weight."

I must admit, I found his response disappointing. Until that point, I had never experienced such disparity. As an athlete, I had always been given the benefit of the doubt and received assistance and opportunities. However, now I find myself on the outside looking in, even after a successful career. It was disheartening to realize that even a person who was coaching Division I football couldn't help me by making a call to someone they knew on another Division I staff. Nevertheless, the lesson I learned from that situation, which I now want to pass on to you, is the importance of finding people who know you and are willing to make a call or offer you a job, regardless of your level of experience.

Almost every Football staff will prioritize recruiting as the number one thing they look for when hiring coaches. The funny thing is, while we're playing professional football, there are young men who transmon from being undergraduates to becoming student managers on football teams. These student managers then become graduate assistants, and it is their ability to thrive in high- pressure environments under different types of **leadership** that ultimately gets them hired. They are willing to do whatever it takes and fulfill any task assigned to them. This means that a graduate assistant from the University of Tennessee, who never played football but started as a student manager, may secure a coaching job before someone who played professional football for ten years and has five years of coaching experience. I hate to admit it, but that's just the reality of the situation. It's not a matter of race; it's about the career path you choose. This system often leads one to question, "Should I have left football earlier? Should I have gone back and become a graduate assistant?" You only have a seven-year window. Once you graduate from college or finish playing college football, you have only seven years to become a graduate assistant.

In my case, I played for ten years, so by the time I finished playing, my opportunity to be a GA had passed, and I could only volunteer or be hired in a position with restricted earnings.

Don't get me wrong, I am extremely grateful to the coaches who helped me learn how to coach, but I also appreciate that they showed me what the other side of the coin looked like. What I find peculiar is that some of those coaches didn't really know how to coach the positions they were assigned to, and there were even coaches who weighed 300 pounds. There were individuals coaching wide receivers who played defensive line in high school. However, because they were exposed to the right teachings and had the right networks and connections by being around non- minorities, they were able to secure coaching jobs. That's why it is crucial to develop and nurture the right associations when you're looking for a job as a coach.

Attitude

Your attitude plays a crucial role in determining how coachable you are, and if you want to succeed in your post-sports career, it is essential to constantly assess and adjust your attitude. As a player, I was highly receptive to coaching. However, once I stopped playing, I initially didn't see the need for further coaching. Nevertheless, I had mentors *who* continued to teach me valuable lessons, such as the importance of body language in an interview. They advised me on things like not wearing earrings and sitting upright and forward, as sitting back could convey a lack of interest. These mentors equipped me with different types of body language that would allow me to present myself confidently and assertively during interviews.

Your attitude during an interview plays a significant role in *how* you are perceived and can greatly impact the outcome. How you present yourself in an interview is crucial in securing a job. Personally, I always make sure to present myself in a clean-cut manner, wearing a shirt and tie. I use polite language like "Yes sir" and "No sir," and I respond to questions directly instead of overwhelming the interviewer with excessive knowledge. Speaking too much during an interview can sometimes give the impression that you think you know it all. I do understand that most coaching staff seek new coaches *who* can thrive under their guidance and within their systems. They're looking at your attitude to determine if you will fit in as an integral part of their coaching staff. It's important not to come across as the guy *who* will try to take their job.

Being coachable means being willing to demonstrate leadership, being open to receiving constructive criticism, being ready to take on additional responsibilities, and being able to handle losses with resilience while maintaining a servant leadership mindset.

After nine years of coaching, I reached the pinnacle of my career as the defensive coordinator for the Montreal Alouettes in the CFL. It was a prestigious position, and I was particularly thrilled because I spoke French and had ascended to the role of defensive coordinator faster than many of my peers. I earned a degree in public administration with a focus on executive leadership, which taught me a great deal about how to lead. However, I realized that my education had not provided me with enough knowledge on how to follow. I kept hearing the term "servant leader."

In I 904, Robert K. Greenleaf defined servant leadership as follows: "The servant-leader is servant first...It begins with the natural feeling that one wants to serve, to serve first." I discovered that being a servant leader also meant following the people I lead. It involves serving them through various means and methods. While I have always been a strong and assertive leader, which I believe is necessary, I also understand that some individuals prefer a humbler approach. They want a leader who serves others, who steps down from a position of authority, and who leads with character and integrity. Although I already possess those two qualities, I learned in time that to be a coach was to *lead,* the way a General would lead an army.

Most of the defensive coordinators I had the opportunity to play for or work with were older white men who had the autonomy to run their programs as they saw fit. They pushed me to my limits, yelling, cursing, challenging me, and even name- calling. However, it was these men who left the strongest impression on me, as they played a significant role in shaping me into an elite athlete. I was fortunate to have driven individuals who pushed me to the brink of exhaustion, allowing me to bounce back with renewed enthusiasm and effort. This approach served me well as a player, and when I transitioned into coaching, I tried to emulate their style. However, I soon realized that this approach didn't resonate with everyone. Personally, it wasn't the kind of coach I wanted to be. Nonetheless, I maintained a mindset of learning, absorbing everything around me, and applying the lessons I had learned. Little did I know that I was about to receive a coaching lesson from someone I consider the epitome of a football coach.

During the 2012-20!3 seasons, I had the privilege of coaching under Chris Creighton at Drake University. Chris was a deeply devout Christian man who exuded energy, happiness, positivity, insight, and inspiration all at once. He coached without resorting to cursing, demeaning, or negative criticism. Instead, he motivated and coached with love. This didn't mean he didn't challenge his players; rather, his approach involved saying things like, "I know you can do better; I believe in you, I need you to knock that guard down!"

Here I was, in the middle of my coaching career, being profoundly inspired by a man of faith. Chris's attitude exemplified excellence in every aspect. I coached under him for two years, but I must confess that as soon as I reached the professional level, I reverted to the familiar habits of running a team like a business, employing an overly strict approach. Needless to say, I fell back into the wrong mindset and attitude.

If you want to secure a coaching job at a university, it is important to do your homework beforehand. Prior to the interview, take the time to research the school or team you aspire to coach for. Study their historical traditions and demographics. Pay attention to the coach's demeanor and habits. When you arrive for the interview, observe your surroundings and make note of anything unusual to demonstrate your attentiveness.

I always bring a resume to interviews, highlighting my coaching experience at all levels: high school, college, and professional. During the interview, I am mindful of the person I may potentially work for. I assess if I can fit into their coaching puzzle and if it is a mutually beneficial fit. I make sure to arrive on time, or even a little early. I respond promptly when spoken to. These seemingly simple actions can make a significant difference and set you apart from other candidates. It shows your ability to lead when given the opportunity, take initiative, and make those around you feel comfortable. As someone with a lengthy playing and coaching background, it is easy to intimidate a student manager who may feel their job is at risk if you are hired.

Being sociable is crucial. A colleague once told me, "If I can't have a drink with you, I can't work with you." Although I wasn't a drinker, after being hired, I made an effort to act as the designated driver. I would occasionally have a beer, emphasizing that it was just one beer and taking my time to drink it. If the coaching group was doing shots, I would take the first shot and then fill my shot glass with Coke or Pepsi, so I appeared to be participating. However, there were times when I had to fit in, like another piece of the puzzle. Whether or not you enjoy these social activities, gaining the trust of your colleagues is crucial. When they know they can trust and work with you, it becomes easier to navigate situations where your character or faith may differ from that of the group. I'm not suggesting compromising your beliefs but acknowledging that finding the right job requires careful consideration of your attitude and how you approach fitting into the team dynamic.

Appearance

I've briefly discussed appearance, but now let's delve deeper into how you should present yourself. I was always taught to maintain a clean-cut look, without earrings, mustaches, or excessive facial hair. It's important to be as dean-shaven as possible, almost resembling military personnel. This demonstrates a focused intent towards your job and professionalism. As a player, I had a flashy and showy persona, but that didn't align well with many of the coaches I worked for, as they didn't promote that kind of environment. Consequently, I clashed with several coaches and had to learn to tone it down. You learn which individuals you need to dial back your energy with, as they may not be capable of handling such exuberance.

Another aspect of the hiring hierarchy is the pigeonholing of minority coaches, particularly African American coaches, into certain positions such as running back coach, wide receiver coach, defensive back coach, or D-line coach. There are very few African-American offensive coordinators, quarterback coaches, head coaches, general managers, and currently, no African-American majority team owners in the NFL. In an environment where African American players make up the majority, being a constant minority can make it challenging to find the right job fit. The NFL has implemented the Rooney Rule, which mandates teams to interview a certain number of African-American candidates. While this is both good and bad for us, perhaps one day, the pendulum will swing in our favor. Regardless, the same principles still apply to appearance, attitude, and association. These factors heavily influence your chances of finding a job.

In addition to the top three principles, I believe attending coaching clinics and conventions, actively promoting your resume to schools at every level, and accepting jobs that align with your family's needs are also crucial factors in getting hired as a coach.

Before I get into discussing how to maintain a job, there is one critical point I want to emphasize. If you are a current player looking to transition into a coaching career, or if you are just starting your professional playing career, I have a simple yet challenging bonus tip for you: listen up! Take advantage of seminars that provide guidance on handling your finances. Don't view these educational meetings as just another mandatory obligation. If you neglected to pay attention during your time in university, now is the time to gain a solid understanding, especially when it comes to managing your finances.

During my playing days, I was spending two- to three- hundred dollars a day on shopping, food, alcohol, and clubbing. I was splurging a significant amount of money on having fun. Imagine if I had invested that money to secure my future. One suggestion I have is to pair each rookie at the professional level with a veteran or retired player. Additionally, I believe rookies should be required to complete a certain number of hours of financial management classes. Once individuals are equipped with knowledge, they tend to make better decisions. Even those who are aware of financial management can still fall victim to scams or mismanagement of their money, so there is no perfect system in place. Players will spend their money on lavish cars, houses, women, drugs, recreational toys, trips, clothes, and everything else they desire.

There's a famous line from the movie "Baby Boy" that goes, "Gunz and Butta." "Butta" represents flashy and extravagant items like cars, clothes, and jewelry, while "Gunz" represents real estate, stocks, bonds, and artwork - things that appreciate in value over a lifetime.

In conclusion, smart players never stop educating themselves and consistently work on improving their associations, attitudes, and appearances.

Part IX - How to Keep a Job

Okay, so now you're familiar with those four amazing words, "When can you start?" You leap about fifty feet in the air, let out a wild scream, and immediately call and text everyone you know to share the fantastic news. But then, for a moment, you find yourself holding your breath. Your mind starts racing at a rapid pace. You question whether you truly have what it takes to meet the expectations. While you're thrilled, a hint of apprehension dampens your excitement. Now, what should you do? How do you *maintain* this job, this incredible opportunity that has been granted to you due to your hard work, determination, and perseverance?

I call them the Three P's:

I. Preparation

2. Performance

3. Professionalism

Now, let's get into them...

Preparation

When you're prepared spiritually, mentally, emotionally, and physically, you're prepared for success. As someone who doesn't drink coffee, the first thing I do in the morning is dedicate time to prayer and quiet reflection to align my spirit and mind for the day ahead. I offer prayers for the health and safety of my family and myself, as well as for those who rely on me to succeed. Football at the professional and college levels is a serious business, with high expectations academically, athletically, and socially. Your role, regardless of the level, is to get the job done, perform at your best, or face the consequences. And that requires preparation.

Your daily preparation and plan for success are half the battle. The other part is executing that plan consistently despite the challenges you may face, such as the diverse staff, the diversity among your students, and the circumstances that arise within the family structures of the players you coach.

I once had a star player at the professional level who got arrested for drugs. I took a risk and vouched for him to the coaching staff and ownership group. I firmly believed that there was more to the story and that we should investigate before dismissing him. It turned out that he was associated with someone involved in selling drugs, and the police were pressuring him to cooperate. I stood up for this player, and we didn't release him. He ended up making a significant impact the following year and became an All-Star. He eventually retired as one of the top players in the Canadian Football League.

Building relationships is an essential part of preparing to be great. I have always sought to develop meaningful connections with players, just as I did with the young man I mentioned earlier. I believe that's why they refer to me as a player's coach. However, advocating for players can be risky, as some coaches may warn you that certain players can undermine your position or harm the team's dynamics. Therefore, every day requires preparation to navigate these different dynamics, and each situation demands a suitable approach when dealing with the player in front of you. Sometimes, a firm and straightforward coach face is necessary, strictly focused on business. Other times, you must assume the role of a counselor when players face issues with their spouses, children, legal matters, substance abuse, depression, or other challenges.

Occasionally, you need to be a father figure, setting an example of how a man should handle certain situations. And sometimes, you stand beside them as a friend, offering motivation and support without judgment. Properly preparing yourself will enable you to be ready when you are needed and to understand and connect with your players daily.

It's important to keep in mind that the world of football is driven by ego, and this applies not only to players but also to coaches. Among coaches, there exists a wide spectrum of dynamics. Some have played football, and some haven't. Some express these feelings in very jealous ways and choose to manipulate these feelings of inadequacy on decision-makers and close associates. It could be that one coach is being considered for a head coaching position or receiving media recognition while others are not. With so many variables in play within a team, it can be surprising that teams manage to maintain unity, often relying on slogans like "great things happen when no one cares or gets the credit" to bring them together and keep egos in check. However, the strength of a team ultimately relies on its leader. If a leader is chaotic or overly authoritarian, it can lead to disarray. On the other hand, if a leader is too weak, chaos can also ensue. Striking the right balance is crucial, requiring a strong head coach who can effectively manage leaders, including ownership, while also being accessible and supportive to the players.

My former Defensive Coordinator and friend, Devone Claybrooks, once gave me this perspective, "When you become a head coach, *then* you can do it your way. Until then, you must make the best of what you are given. Personally, I never fully accepted this idea because I believed I was an exceptional football coach with answers to every question. After all, that's how you rise to the top. You ascend by having solutions to every problem. Being result-oriented is crucial. Many coaches solely pursue championships. I find myself torn on this matter because my initial motivation for coaching was to win championships, develop players, improve their skills, and help them succeed financially. That's what I was taught. On the other hand, there are coaches whose goal is not solely about championships. They focus on shaping players, building character, and promoting integrity. Ideally, both aspects should be present in every coach, but unfortunately, that's not always the case. Throughout my life, I have always strived to win in everything I do. In the realm of professional sports, winning is a direct result of doing things the right way. You win by executing tasks correctly, treating people with respect, winning over fans, and running a successful business.

As I grow older and transition from one job to another, I have come to understand that there are different ways to win and lose. I don't have to win every game or every championship. The true championship lies in winning relationships, in winning the support of the people around me, and in winning with my family.

Professionalism

To me, professionalism means being accountable. As a coach, you are responsible for numerous aspects: how your work is presented, prepared, executed, and implemented. It also includes your interactions with colleagues, your demeanor at work, and even your conduct outside of work, such as drinking or road rage. The professionalism of a coach encompasses a wide range of factors because, to be honest, you are always representing your role. You don't get to switch it off when you're at the grocery store and find yourself in an argument with the cashier. Due to the visibility of your occupation, you always have to be mindful that someone, somewhere, is watching and observing you. If they witness you behaving inappropriately, they may share it with others, even on social media platforms. I understand that it may seem unfair at times, resembling the life of a celebrity where paparazzi constantly follow you, leaving you with little privacy and the inability to simply be a human being. Coaching is both a gift and a curse, but when you choose this line of work, you sign up for it whether you like it or not.

I believe that professionalism can be perceived differently by different individuals. This is especially true for African Americans who often must maintain professionalism at *all times*. If you let your guard down, even for a moment, the media will be quick to label you as having an attitude, being aggressive, or unprofessional. The unfortunate truth is that white coaches sometimes receive leniency, even if they are rude or distant. Their behavior is very quickly overlooked. On the other hand, if African-American coaches act in the same manner, they are swiftly labeled as unprofessional simply because they don't agree or get along with certain individuals in the office. In my opinion, this is one of the reasons why there are fewer black head coaches. Ownership often doubts whether these individuals can effectively lead the team. Tony Dungy serves as a great example of an African American who embodied professionalism, integrity, and preparedness, but it's important to remember that not everyone can be like Tony Dungy.

Deon Sanders comes to mind as an example. He was a phenomenal player who hesitated to enter coaching because he didn't want to conform to every aspect of the traditional coaching protocol. He didn't want to shave his beard or wear a shirt and tie every day. He wanted to be himself. This is the line that individuals must consider when deciding whether or not to pursue coaching. Are they willing to prioritize professionalism over their individualism? For some people, it's difficult.

Personally, I strive to be around men of high character, and I aim to present myself with high character consistently. However, it is undeniably difficult to do so all the time. Once you determine the level of professionalism required for a particular job, you must be able to conform to it. If you find that you are unable to do so, it may be necessary to seek a different job. Otherwise, you risk bing labeled, which can easily jeopardize your career.

Players have more freedom to express themselves. They can have dreadlocks, wear grills, baggy jeans, or even have certain habits or lifestyles. Players are primarily judged based on their performance, whereas coaches are evaluated based on their ability to excel m three areas: preparation, performance, and professionalism.

When it comes to players, they are coached on the skills and strategies that will contribute to the team's success in games. However, the expectations for coaches are different. You won't see many coaches sporting big beards. If they do have facial hair, it's often a collective team decision, representing unity and solidarity.

Coaches with dreadlocks are also not as commonly accepted. While it may be biased, such appearances are not typically embraced in coaching. The prevailing perception is that coaches should have a clean-cut, well-groomed, and professional appearance to set themselves apart from the players.

So, if you aspire to become a coach, it's important to understand that professionalism and assimilation into the coaching culture are essential. Coaches are expected to uphold certain standards, such as wearing their pants properly and avoiding sagging. I've also learned that coaches are not typically associated with a strong sense of fashion. Personally, I've been called a prima donna because I pay attention to matching my clothing, socks, and ensuring they are clean.

However, the image of coaches is often that of hardcore drill sergeants who prioritize their coaching duties over individual appearance. Despite being a former player and still having those inclinations, I have learned to adapt and assimilate into the coaching culture. I aim to be a coach who possesses the required integrity, character, and professionalism to achieve success. I want to be judged based on my preparation, performance, and professionalism.

Being a true professional sometimes means making sacrifices. For example, you may not be able to kneel during the national anthem, even if you personally want to. As a coach, you may have to stand for the anthem, regardless of whether you agree with it or not, because you have signed up to align with the company line, which may differ from the stance taken by the players.

People often tell me, "Kahlil, you seem wise beyond your years. Your maturity level surpasses that of your peers." I believe that a significant part of who I am as a person has been shaped by experiences of loss. Especially during my playing days, while I enjoyed the game, I also focused on preparing for life after it. Unlike many college students who could be carefree, I was married, had kids, and carried responsibilities. My family depended on me, and I embraced those responsibilities.

Once I retired from playing, I didn't have to wonder about what I would do next. I had a plan. With my degree in hand, I decided to pursue coaching. I had a strong faith in God and felt secure. So, for me, the transition wasn't as challenging, although I recognize that it can be for others.

Now, from the time I retired to where I am now, there have been a lot of struggles and a lot of loss. Finding coaching jobs has been a challenge. I moved to a state where diversity was scarce, and most people were unaware of my past as a superstar African-American athlete. I had to rebuild my identity in a different context and under different circumstances.

Now, I am known for my character, determination, energy, and my relationship with God and my family. People recognize me for these qualities rather than my past as a great football player. This process has contributed to my continued personal growth and maturity. I had to let go of my previous identity as "The People's Champ," a nickname I once had. That version of me is no longer remembered. "Kahlil, the Real Deal", has essentially died, and I had to develop a new persona as Coach Carter. Coach Carter is someone who maintains a professional appearance, wears his pants properly, is well-groomed and articulate, has a strong relationship with God, and remains humble. Through this development, I experienced some losses.

One such loss was a job in Calgary when I chose to change positions after losing the championship. I made this decision because I wanted to be with my family, and I didn't align with the values and principles of the organization. Sometimes, you lose opportunities while finding your way through the world, but the important thing is to be consistent and authentic with who you are.

Coaching in the NFL has always been a dream of mine, especially considering my short stint there as a player. I do believe that I have the potential to succeed as an NFL coach based on my coaching style and the knowledge I possess. However, I recognize the need to bridge the gap between coaching in a way that meets the team's requirements and my own approach as a "player's coach." I would relish the opportunity to coach at the highest level alongside the most exceptional athletes on the planet. Achieving this would be the culmination of all the hard work and sacrifices I have made.

Nevertheless, before signing any contract, it is essential for me to know who I would be working for and understand their philosophies and habits. Since my last job, I made a promise to myself that I would never accept a job out of necessity. Instead, I would only commit to a position that is the right fit for me. I want to work for someone I can genuinely believe in - someone who aligns with my values, coaching style, and dedication to winning and making a positive impact in the community and the world. Additionally, it is crucial that they respect and value what I bring to the table. If I am merely seen as a temporary fill-in, I would not be interested in that job. However, if they see me as an individual who can contribute and help improve the team, I would eagerly join that organization without hesitation. I never want to experience being misunderstood again or work for someone who does not understand or appreciate my beliefs and principles.

Furthermore, in terms of preparation, performance, and professionalism, I would bring these three qualities to any job I am given. In my view, being prepared beyond what is expected is vital at the highest level. This means arriving early, staying late, and being available for players to ask questions. It also means actively listening and learning from other coaches, as one of the greatest advantages of being in the NFL is the opportunity to gain knowledge and insights from successful coaches. If you are not willing to put in the time and effort, and if you only want to go home after a game, then you might as well coach high school.

Part IX - How to Lose a Job

You lose a job almost the same way you get it: Attitude, Professionalism & Performance

Attitude

It's interesting how attitudes can be perceived as negative, even when they come from a place of positivity. Sometimes, being excessively happy can actually make people dislike you, simply because you're "too happy." It's a paradoxical situation. On the other hand, when you respond negatively to bad events, which I admit I do at times, people may question your mental toughness and ability to overcome challenges.

During my coaching tenure in Montreal, I encountered situations where I wasn't allowed to implement strategies that I believed would lead to a successful team. It wasn't anyone's fault, but rather a difference in the way things were done. However, I couldn't help but feel slighted and undervalued, and frustration started to seep in. When I discussed this with my peers, instead of offering guidance on how to handle the situation, they simply agreed with me. This validation fueled my frustration even more.

I must admit that my attitude during that period wasn't the best. Nevertheless, my focus was on being a strong, assertive, knowledgeable, and victorious leader. I wasn't concerned about being offensive, harsh, or inflexible. My sole concern was achieving success in the next game. Therefore, attitude can be both a gift and a curse, particularly when external factors start to affect you emotionally.

Professionalism

When it comes to professionalism, I have always been punctual and ready to work. However, as an African American, I have noticed that certain behaviors or mannerisms can be deemed unprofessional, even if they are acceptable to others. It seems that different individuals are held to different standards. For instance, Donald Trump might get away with certain actions that Barack Obama would have faced severe criticism for. It's the same office but with contrasting outcomes. I have come to appreciate the disparities that exist within African-American culture to a greater extent recently. Previously, I didn't pay much attention or feel that those disparities should apply to me because I knew I was a competent coach. However, I now realize the importance of consistently demonstrating the appropriate level of professionalism and humility towards others. True humility requires acknowledging and respecting the authority placed above you. If you show humility to your family but not to your boss, you will be perceived as lacking humility.

Similarly, if you are humble to the lady at the grocery store but not to firefighters or police officers, your humility is called into question. Learning how to humble yourself is crucial in the realm of professionalism. It is essential to maintain a composed demeanor, especially when dealing with certain individuals, as failing to do so can easily derail all the progress you have made. Some may argue that it means giving up personal power, but I believe it takes more inner strength to humble oneself and remain silent at times than to arrogantly express one's opinions, potentially jeopardizing everything one has worked for.

Am I professional? Absolutely. I am always prepared, punctual, and able to coach any type of player effectively. I treat women with respect. However, all it takes is for someone to misinterpret my actions and say, "Well, he has an attitude. He is unprofessional." Unfortunately, these perceptions can quickly snowball. Attitude and professionalism are closely intertwined, particularly for African Americans. Deviating from these two qualities could potentially cost you a job.

Performance

If you fail to get the job done, whether due to factors like inadequate players, unsuitable schemes, player injuries, changes in ownership, or even personal issues like a divorce, poor performance is one of the quickest paths to losing a job in the results-driven sports industry. For instance, if the offensive coordinator calls a bad play, the quarterback coach might be the first person held accountable, even if the coordinator receives protection from the head coach due to their friendship. The quarterback coach could become the scapegoat. The harsh reality in this business is that sometimes there are scapegoats, and it's unpredictable who will be targeted. When coaching cuts occur, you strive to outperform to ensure that your numbers, statistics, and results shield you. If the head coach or owners fire the offensive coordinator incorrectly, the quarterback coach retains their job. However, if the quarterback coach is fired while the coordinator stays, the powers-that-be may replace both positions and still experience losses, eventually resulting in everyone being fired, including the general manager, for not making the right decision at the right time. Performance is directly connected to success or failure, and it is essential to achieve victories, enhance the brand and organization, or else risk losing your job.

Another way to jeopardize your coaching position is through social media. It's crucial to maintain the same persona on social media as you do as a coach because you are always representing the team. Be cautious when engaging online because people are constantly observing you. Social media can be detrimental to a coach's career, which is why I have largely avoided it, although now that I have a public job again, I use it to promote my events. However, I refrain from liking other people's posts because that often leads to reading the comments. I simply post my event and then log off. Scrolling through social media is not advisable for coaches, as it has proven to be a swift path to job loss, given that one's public persona can be misinterpreted by others.

Additionally, you can risk losing your job if you fail to be a responsible steward over your marriage or neglect your family members. In some cases, family members' actions have led to coaches being fired, as their behavior reflects poorly on the entire organization. Since football is a sport that values family orientation, the people and places involved are intricately connected. I cannot stress enough the importance of demonstrating the same leadership qualities you display on the field to your family. Otherwise, your superiors may perceive you as an inadequate steward of the team as well.

I had a conversation with my brother Aaron, who used to be involved in a gang, regarding his online behavior. I told him, "Aaron, you need to stop with the gangster language and posts. As your brother, I don't want to be associated with that." Similarly, I've had discussions with my daughter about toning down her provocative outfit photos and ensuring she avoids using offensive language or engaging in combative behavior on social media. I remind her that as my daughter, I want her to embody the values of a professional football coach's child, and together, we must uphold our brand. It's crucial that our brand aligns with the character I demonstrate as a coach and the image our team aims to portray as an organization. I emphasize to my entire family, "Once I become a coach, everyone in my family becomes part of the team!"

4th Down:
The iN Crowd

"But when that which is perfect has come, then that which is in part will be done away. When I was a child, I spoke as a child, I understood as a child, I thought as a child; but when I became a man, I put away childish things. For now we see in a mirror, dimly, but then face to face. Now I know in part, but then I shall know just as I also am known."

1 Corinthians 13:10-12

Part X - The African-American Experience

Do you remember the classic show, *D1f Prent Strokes?* Can you imagine the character Arnold, played by Gary Coleman? Well, as a child, I resembled Gary Coleman quite a bit. I was short and chubby, with puffed-out cheeks and light brown eyes. I looked like a plump little chocolate M&M with a big smile and prominent teeth. I would even imitate Arnold's famous line, "Whatchu talkin' 'bout Willis?" and people would burst into laughter.

I discovered my athletic talent at the age of six. Growing up in a household of Redskins fans, Sundays were dedicated to football. Since my birthday fell in September, I joined a club team in Landover, Maryland, at a very young age, and we were actually a pretty talented team. As a short and chubby kid with some athletic ability, I was primarily assigned positions like defensive line, nose guard, and fullback. As I started to slim down a bit, I also got the chance to play wide receiver and serve as the backup quarterback. I could run, manage plays, understand the game, and had good leadership skills. Eventually, I consistently played quarterback and receiver, while occasionally taking on other positions due to my size. I continued playing for the club team until I was about eleven years old when my family moved to Arkansas.

During my childhood, I enjoyed riding bikes and engaging in various sports-related hobbies. We would play bowling, basketball, and football. My brother even dabbled in baseball. It was a different time compared to today, where kids have cell phones filled with games, PlayStations, Netflix, and other sophisticated toys that keep them indoors. When I was young, Atari video games emerged, and playing those games competitively with my brothers only fueled my competitive nature. We would compete in everything!

Despite the presence of drugs and crime in the surrounding area, my brothers and I formed a special bond within our home and neighborhood. I'm happy to say that to this day, most of the kids from our neighborhood remain close. We grew up together and became adults together, although our paths m life took us m different directions.

As I got older, I vividly remember my first day at the University of Arkansas. It was a three-hour trip, although sometimes we would take the two-and-a-half-hour route known as the pig trail, which passed through Harrison, where the headquarters of the Ku Klux Klan was located. For safety reasons, we usually opted for the three-hour trip.

Arkansas is a very racially divided state. There are elites, a substantial middle-class, and a large population of impoverished individuals. Many of the poor are minorities and marginalized citizens in general. Just being in Arkansas, I often felt like a minority. Out of the 40,000 students at the University of Arkansas, only about fifteen percent were African American. However, this racial divide was common across the country, particularly in major Division One universities. As a result, we often gathered within our own sub-communities, meeting in specific areas, eating at certain times, and hosting our own parties. We formed a subculture within the school. I recall a Ku Klux Klan rally during my freshman year when members of the organization walked through our campus, as their headquarters was in close proximity.

The air of tension on campus was heavy, like the thick skin of an elephant. Having come from Little Rock Central High School, where I had experienced similar tension, I could feel it rippling through my core. It wasn't until my time at the University of Arkansas that I faced full-on racism. One year, a few guys jumped out of a car and hurled racial slurs at me - the N-word, darky, and monkey. I tried my best to defend myself, but they managed to rough me up with their hits and kicks. Thankfully, I wasn't seriously injured, but it left me feeling angry and fearful. It made me realize that this kind of incident could happen to me at any time, in any place. Despite what happened, I never told anyone not the police, not my floor's resident advisor, not even the coaches. I had been in Arkansas long enough to understand that sometimes these things happen, and getting roughed up was just a part of it. However, I also recognized that my situation could have turned out much worse. There could have been gun violence, and I could have been seriously harmed. This incident taught me a valuable lesson. It taught me that in similar situations in the future, trying to act tough would likely lead to a tragic outcome.

Back in 1995, when I first started college, a John Singleton movie called "Higher Learning" was released. In one scene, other races were shown attacking minorities and interracial couples on a college campus. W arching that movie or reading its manuscript felt like reliving my own college experience. I could feel the sting of being away from home for the first time, knowing that I couldn't just run back whenever I wanted. I felt like an outsider, a minority in a predominantly white school, like a small piece of a big puzzle that I didn't have all the pieces to. Despite these challenges, I remained determined to make a difference.

Eventually, my fear and apprehension began to fade away, replaced by a sense of relief and excitement when I found out that I would be a part of the U of A football team. You should have seen me! I walked around that campus with a newfound confidence, feeling like I had truly made it - and I had! The campus was stunning, the stadium was breathtaking, and on top of that, U of A was a Division One football school. I had finally escaped the confines of my old neighborhood, and I called this experience "hood to good." I finally felt like I belonged to the "in crowd." I was prepared for the hard work that lay ahead. My university journey had begun, and I was determined to overcome any obstacles-even racism.

Racism

I understand racism as both a social and an ignorance condition. People are often taught a certain way of thinking, and they remain trapped in that belief system throughout their lives. They fail to seek education or experiences that would enable their growth, and as a result, they remain ignorant and unwilling to change. Furthermore, they pass on this same mentality to their children, perpetuating the cycle of ignorance across generations. People tend to be comfortable in their established belief systems and mindsets, resisting any attempt to challenge or break through the generational "system" that exists in their minds, similar to the stagnant nature of the Dead Sea.

The Dead Sea is referred to as "dead" due to its high saltwater content, which prevents fish and aquatic plants from surviving. I refuse to be stagnant like the Dead Sea. I refuse to hinder my personal growth and allow bitterness, anger, and hostility to thrive within me. No way!

My wife is white, and my children are biracial, although my first children are black. This means that I have had a wide range of experiences and diverse opportunities for personal growth. While I am not particularly involved in politics, I am socially aware, and I will never allow discrimination to affect me. I truly believe that this is why I have been able to maintain a balanced perspective on the events around me and continue to evolve as a human being.

You see, growth doesn't just happen by chance. It must be actively pursued. We all age, but aging does not necessarily equate to personal growth and maturity. We must actively seek out opportunities for growth, whether through education, experiencing different countries, languages, and cultures, or even by forming relationships or friendships with people outside of our comfort zones. I refuse to remain the same person I was as a child or a young adult. I am determined to become the person that God intends me to be, as He has created me to be a beacon of light. And a true beacon of light encompasses every color within it.

Handling the Haters

I used to feel the need to engage in every battle or conflict, whether it was related to race or not, that came my way, and it had a negative impact on my interpersonal relationships for a long time. However, I am now realizing that the people who cause me the most problems or criticize me are not worth my energy and attention in the first place. It feels strange for me to say this, as I am naturally inclined to communicate and engage with others. Regardless of someone's status, color, age, or any other factor, I have always been willing to communicate with them in some way. However, I have come to understand that this mindset can put me in a vulnerable position at times.

These days, my motto is to focus on doing the next thing right. When I stumble or make a mistake, my goal is to rectify the situation and make the right choices moving forward, so that I can stay on the path that I am meant to follow.

Part XI - Take It Like A Man (player/coach)

Some men who entered my life through football had the opportunity to guide and influence me as a young man who was in desperate need of direction and guidance. Coach Fitzgerald Hill was one of those men. He served as the wide receiver coach at Arkansas during my time there. He was an African-American man who was deeply involved in community outreach and had a strong passion for football. He was also a highly respected veteran of the armed services, and he was married with a special needs child. Coach Fitzgerald embodied black excellence and was an astute individual. When I became a wide receiver under his guidance, he had the chance to mentor me. He was aware that I had a child, that my mother struggled with drug addiction, and that I faced academic challenges at school. However, he did nothing to assist me in navigating these difficult life situations. The fact that he chose not to help me gain a better understanding of my circumstances troubled me for a long time.

When I first began coaching, I met with Coach Fitzgerald and received some valuable advice that has shaped me into the coach I am today. However, he missed the opportunity to guide a young person towards success in life. Throughout my professional career, I would reach out to him, seeking his feedback and thoughts on my football performance. However, he would not respond or provide any guidance. I felt as though he may have been embarrassed about not taking advantage of the opportunity to help me. One day, I called him and expressed my frustration, saying, "Coach Fitzgerald, you knew the challenges I faced as a young man, and yet you stood on the sidelines, watching me struggle. You could have guided me through the maze of circumstances I was dealing with." I continued, "A mutual friend told me that I need to let go and forgive you because when I needed a father figure who understood the experiences of an African-American athlete, you never cared enough to reach out." I do not recall his response, but finally expressing my long-held resentment was a relief. Like my own father, I have made the decision to be nothing like Fitzgerald

Hill. As a coach, I genuinely care about my players and their lives, not just their performance on the field.

One of the young men I coached, Tanner Varner, acknowledged, "Kahlil is a genuinely good person who is willing to do anything for me. He coaches and supports young athletes, not just in football but in life as well."

Tanner, like every player I have coached, understands that I am committed to helping them become not only better players but also better individuals. This is one of the main reasons why I chose to become a coach, to shape and guide young men. I have learned that Coach Fitzgerald Hill has since earned a doctorate and now assists many former athletes with their personal issues and legal problems. It seems like he is now doing what he should have been doing when I played for him. Unfortunately, he was not there for me. When I have spoken to former teammates, they often describe Coach Hill as being like a father figure to them. I can't help but respond with surprise, thinking, "He was a father to you?"

However, I must remember that the person who said that was on scholarship. Coach Hill did not care about me because I was a walk-on, even though I needed his support even more than the scholarship players. At the time, I was doing my best to stay afloat and maintain academic success, but he did not recognize or perhaps simply did not care about my struggles. He has never explained his actions, and even when I approached him as an adult, he had very little to say. I told him that I wanted him to be a part of my successes, and all he needed to say was, "You know what, Kahlil, I made a mistake. You have made me so proud. You have achieved everything you set out to accomplish. I am proud to have been your coach. I wish I had known the kind of player you would become." Those were the words I needed to hear, but they never came. This motivated me to change the course of my own journey.

Having a father figure in your life helps shape your identity as a man, and I make it a priority to fulfill that role for my players. When you reach the age of fifty, sixty, or even seventy, and you have been away from the game for a long time, you reflect on the relationships you failed to mend or the ones you broke, and in the twilight of your life, you want to reach out. However, the young men you could have helped are now too far removed from the point where you could have made a difference in their lives. I never want to be that far removed or out of touch.

Many of my players still reach out to me, even years after they have left my team, just to say hello or seek advice. My wife asks, "Why are you always answering those calls?" I say, "Because that was me at that age. That young man might need to talk to me, he might need some help-and I'm going to be there for him, no matter what."

When I left coaching, my family life improved drastically, more than I could have ever imagined. My wife experienced less stress because I was at home with her, rather than in a far-off country where we could only see each other every thirty to forty days. That's the first point. Secondly, I am here to support my wife in raising and teaching our children, disciplining them, loving them, praying for them, praying with them, and being present in their lives. I am here every day to share the responsibility of parenting and be the husband my wife needs. She has come to realize that coaching skills are still valuable, even at home. I am now able to manage our finances, and we even bought a house.

Moreover, my two older kids from my first marriage can now spend more time with me during the season. When I was coaching, there were about eight months when I was not very accessible to them. Between meetings, practice, events, and being in another country, I couldn't see them. However, now my daughters and I can Skype and talk to each other every day, as well as on the weekends when I don't have games. It feels incredible to have an abundance of time available for them, and our relationship has blossomed much more than it did in the last two years when I was coaching.

My relationship with God is also back on track, which wasn't the case in Canada. Canada is a very different place when it comes to religion. It's not like there are Baptist, Catholic, and Lutheran churches everywhere. They have different types of churches as well as different types of religions, and there are many atheists in Canada. With the country having a somewhat French influence, you quickly learn that the French use blasphemy to curse. In Quebec, they say "Esti de tabarnak de calice." So "esti" is like the body of Christ, the flesh, like the communion. "T abernac" refers to the actual church. "Calice" is like the Holy Grail or the blood of Christ, the chalice. Therefore, when they curse, saying that phrase is like saying, "FU MF'er, you're a holy mess." It's the worst form of cursing. In Quebec, they use the church and the body of Christ to curse. It's not a very religious region, so being away from Canada has restored my relationship with God to a more balanced and solid state. I started attending church more frequently and eventually took a job as the Sports Ministry Director. It was wonderful because I was constantly surrounded by godly people, and that was instrumental in my personal and spiritual healing process.

People who have heard me speak often compare me to Eric Thomas, also known as the hip-hop preacher. During his motivational speeches, he often emphasizes the importance of wanting success more than anything else, even more than the need to breathe. People say that my voice and mannerisms resemble his. One day, I aspire to speak at the NFL Rookie Symposium and provide valuable insights to the rookies entering the league about the risks and rewards of their behavior.

If given the opportunity, I would tell them, "Being your mother's son is still the best way to go. Having an inflated ego is going to cause you issues, because, eventually, you're going to have to go back to being your momma's son. At some point, whether you get it, got it, or don't get it or got it, *1t* gets you. Make sense? If you act like a fool, you're going to have to return to that place where you started. Broke or rich, it doesn't matter. God is going to bring you to your knees in surrender. Why not be consistent with who you've always been after you get the money and the fame? That's the way the greats do it. They maintain their authenticity throughout the process. Remember, when life changes, it doesn't mean you have to ... except for the better."

Overtime:
The Next Chapter

"No weapon formed against you shall prosper, and every tongue which rises against you in judgment you shall condemn. This is the heritage of the servants of the Lord, and their righteousness is from Me," says the Lord. "

Isaiah 54:17

"Finally, my brethren, be strong in the Lord and in the power of His might. Put on the whole armor of God that you may be able to stand against the wiles of the devil. For we do not wrestle against flesh and blood, but against principalities, against powers, against the rulers of the darkness of this age, against spiritual hosts of wickedness in the heavenly places. Therefore, take up the whole armor of God that you may be able to withstand in the evil day, and having done all, to stand.

Stand therefore, having girded your waist with truth, having put on the breastplate of righteousness, and having shod your feet with the preparation of the gospel of peace; above all, taking the shield of faith with which you will be able to quench all the fiery darts of the wicked one. And take the helmet of salvation, and the sword of the Spirit, which is the word of God; praying always with all prayer and supplication in the Spirit, being watchful to this end with all perseverance and supplication for all the saints."
Ephesians 6:10-18

Part XII - Reflection

My path isn't for everyone. Sports aren't for everyone. Each one of us needs to embark on the journey to become who we are meant to be. No one else can walk your path. It is uniquely yours to navigate, as God has a plan for each and every one of us. It has been said that if you want to make God laugh, tell him your plans. Having faith means trusting that God will guide you to where he intends you to be and orchestrating the timing of it all. It also means being spiritually aware enough to recognize what steps to take once you arrive there. In my opinion, that is what living an **iNfluential** life is all about.

The Principles of Success

The success I have achieved is a direct result of implementing the lessons I learned from all the coaches I had the opportunity to play under throughout my long career. I was always eager to absorb knowledge, and I am elated to say that I possess a photographic memory.

In my opinion, football serves a purpose as long as it is played with integrity. I consider myself blessed to have not only sharpened my skills but also enhanced my overall understanding of the game under the guidance of a diverse range of teachers and coaches. They imparted to me the fundamental principles and nuances essential for achieving success. Here are a few:

1.   One of the most crucial principles I acquired 1s the realization that football does not love you back. Mark T restman conveyed this sentiment to me during my time with the Montreal Alouettes. Despite our immense passion for the game, it continuously demands from us until it decides our time is up. Therefore, it is vital to extract something valuable from the game, be it financial gain, spiritual growth, meaningful relationships, or any other form of benefit, as it can abruptly conclude in the blink of an eye.

2. Play the game with class. I firmly believe that fair play is the epitome of good sportsmanship, and as such, I have never intentionally sought to harm an opposing team member. I have never been one to engage in excessive chatter during games. However, if someone acted foolishly, unprofessionally, or posed a danger, regardless of whether they were my teammate or opponent, I might have addressed the situation. Nonetheless, I have always maintained a demeanor of class on the field. I strongly believe that playing the game fairly is not only the best approach but also the only way I could play it.

3.   The game of football is about relationships. Not about fame, not about money, not about any of those things. It's about the bonds formed with the individuals in the locker room that extend far beyond the field. These are the same individuals who may stand by your side on occasions like your wedding, funeral, or even your bar mitzvah. My teammates are the ones who have made every moment of playing the game truly worthwhile. Even if one never wins a championship but gains a hundred friends, they can genuinely be considered champions. This invaluable principle was imparted to me by Coach Pinball Clemons, who coached me in Toronto for three years.

4.   I believe that football is God's game. In my belief, God is omnipresent and omrnsc1ent, ex1stmg everywhere and possessing all knowledge and insight. While His presence is pervasive, I hold the belief that football holds a special place in

His heart due to the qualities it encompasses: honor, passion, spirituality, and excitement. Nevertheless, it is important to acknowledge that not everyone recognizes, possesses, or requires these attributes. I perceive those who participate in football as God's gladiators, and that is why I have always been actively involved with the Fellowship of Christian Athletes (FCA). Through outreach efforts and utilizing my platform, I strive to convey God's message, as He has bestowed upon me immense blessings through this game.

5. Heavy is the head that wears the crown. Although William Shakespeare utilized it in his play, King Henry IV, with slight modification, the phrase "uneasy lies the head that wears a crown" carries the connotation that a person in a position of authority or leadership bears numerous responsibilities, making their role challenging. They have the power to influence others to do both right and wrong. King Henry expresses the discomfort and burden that the crown brings, preventing him from finding restful sleep.

Similarly, as an athlete, when you find yourself in such a position, you automatically become a role model, whether or not you consciously intend to be. I frequently encounter arguments from both sides of this debate. Some guys just don't want to be role models, while some guys pretend to be and are not. It's a fine line to walk when you're an athlete in the public eye.

When we choose to pursue careers as professional athletes, we willingly accept everything that comes with it: constant media attention, invasion of privacy, public disclosure of salaries, and even personal conflicts with significant others. All these responsibilities and dramas come hand in hand with the title. That is precisely why I have always chosen to play the game with fairness. I have consciously steered clear of negative media attention and have consistently dedicated myself to helping my community and striving for excellence. Through the game, I have gained immeasurable benefits. While it has taken a toll on my physical health, I have received abundant blessings from God in terms of relationships, spirituality, and social connections. These rewards were enough to keep me playing for as long as I did.

6. Football is a privilege one must work for. Luke 12:48 says, "To whom much is given, much is required." Having the opportunity to play collegiate football, even without a scholarship, was a blessing and a privilege. I never felt entitled to the opportunities that were bestowed upon me. When I transitioned to the professional level, I played with a hunger for more, sometimes feeling unsatisfied with the level of success I had achieved. I constantly explored different teams, leagues, and coaches in search of the right fit for my growth. My focus was always on personal improvement rather than mere contentment or happiness. My life's mission has always been to strive to be better than I was yesterday and to surpass my current self tomorrow.

I have always been aware of the tremendous responsibility that comes with what I do, which is why I have made it a priority to give back. I have consistently felt blessed in life. If my life were a movie, it could aptly be titled "Blessed Beyond Measure." Properly aligning your priorities is crucial, as it determines whether you find yourself at the mercy of negative social media attention, the barrel of a police officer's firearm, or the judgment of a court. When your priorities are in order, it becomes easier to discern who is truly supportive and who is not. As Psalm I:I states, "Blessed is the man who does not walk in the counsel of the wicked." By distancing yourself from negative influences and distractions, you greatly increase your chances of living a fulfilling life and enjoying the privilege of participating in God's game.

Proverbs 18:16 further emphasizes the impact of one's talents, stating that "A man's gift makes room for him and brings him before great men." I have witnessed this principle in action within the football world. Your talent not only gamers recognition but also brings you in front of influential individuals, creating opportunities for advancement. In fact, your talent creates as much space for you as you are willing to explore and pursue.

Regrets

Do I have any regrets about my playing career?

Sure, a couple. Firstly, I did not apply for the draft after my rookie season. I think you're allowed a certain amount of time after starting your pro football career to go into a supplemental draft, and after my first year in 2000, I was a pretty good athlete, and I had learned a lot about football. And even after my second year, which was in 2001, there was still a window for me to jump into the draft. I was strong and I was fast; I was talented, young, and hungry. I probably should've gone into the NFL draft at that point, just to have the chance to work out for teams and show them what I could do. That experience would have been really advantageous to my career.

Secondly, of course, I wish I hadn't played in that flag football game and injured my groin because it derailed my NFL career. Giving back to my community ended up costing me an opportunity to play for the NFL's number one defense after having a great NFL Europe campaign. The NFL was excited about me; they even left a spot open for me. The Buffalo Bills did not draft a defensive back in any of the early rounds because they had me in NFL Europe. I regret not being able to capitalize on that opportunity, especially after the hard work I did to be successful.

Other than that, I think that the things that happened along the way happened the way they were supposed to. I played in a lot of leagues, I played a lot of football, and I got to meet a lot of great people. I was on television a bunch. I made some video games. I made my mom, family, and friends proud. I was able to get my degree. On top of all that, while I was starting my pro-football career, my marriage was very sound, and I had some great kids. I believe that how you respond to life prepares you for what it dishes out next. One experience builds on another. The storms, injuries, and our unique circumstances mold and shape us into who we're supposed to become.

Part XIII - Recovery

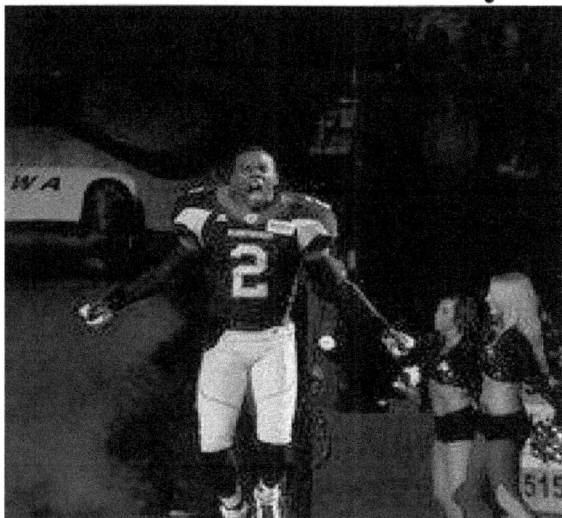

There are three key points I want to emphasize in this chapter. It is important to me that you take these points to heart, as my teachings are based on a wealth of experience and wisdom. First and foremost, I want to stress the significance of servant-leadership. The best leaders are those who prioritize serving others rather than seeking personal promotion. This concept is beautifully articulated by Spencer Conley in his book "Lead with L.O.V.E.," where he states, "Your behavior makes you a leader, not your tide."

Secondly, I urge you to learn from your past experiences and use that knowledge to shape a future that is both feasible and executable. It is vital to reflect on your mistakes and successes in order to grow and progress.

Lastly, regardless of the failures or setbacks you encounter in life, it is crucial to seek solace and guidance from God. He has the power to restore you and lead you towards a fulfilling life, provided you align your steps with His. Personally, I believe that even if I never coach again, I am still equipped to excel in other areas of life. I am educated and blessed with a wonderful family. If coaching is not part of God's plan for my life, I am content with that. However, as a human being and a child of God, I have experienced restoration and renewal by seeking Him out. This newfound sense of wholeness empowers me to tackle any job with humility and achieve great success, while also building lasting relationships along the way.

When I contemplate the concept of "recovery," my mind often turns to Alcoholics Anonymous (AA) and its twelve-step program. Just as alcoholism is a form of addiction, ego can also become a destructive force that hinders personal growth. It is akin to a drug, as it compels you to control every aspect of your life. However, the ultimate truth is that God is in control. By surrendering and allowing God to guide your path, you can avoid stumbling and find glory and victory, even when things don't go according to plan. This aligns with the popular saying, "Let go and let God." During my coaching career, I used to try to orchestrate my own desired outcomes and scenarios to secure victory. However, this approach only added unnecessary pressure and often overlooked the fact that other individuals had influence over the situation and its outcome.

If I were to decide to coach another team in the future, I would have learned enough to prioritize my values in the correct order: faith, family, and then football. There have been instances where I have had to sever relationships that were one-sided or contentious due to these priorities. However, before taking such actions, I always conduct a self-inventory and reflect on my own behavior. I ask myself, "What could I have done better? How did I contribute to the situation?" If I identify any flaws in my own conduct, I make it a point to rectify them by approaching the person involved and making amends. This ability to take responsibility for my actions and seek reconciliation has been a significant area of personal growth that I take pride in. As I have continued to mature, I have acquired more effective and efficient tools in my tool belt.

As a coach, your tool belt must encompass a wide range of experiences that have shaped you into who you are today, right at this very moment. In addition to these experiences, other crucial tools include strength, confidence, intelligence, and humility. It is important to constantly adjust and refine your tool belt, adding new tools and discarding ones that are no longer useful. After all, as coaches, our main focus is on building various things - be it businesses, individuals, or products. By ensuring that we have the right tools at our disposal, every coach has the potential to become a master builder.

Part XIV - Rewards

So, now that you've read the story of a young person facing challenges and overcoming them, you understand the importance of staying faithful. You've also learned about a man who managed to escape his environment, achieve success as a football player, and become a coach and mentor. But my story is far from over, and I'm starting to see the rewards of the way I've lived my life.

God, in His faithfulness, continues to guide me. To be honest, I've become more cautious in recent years, carefully choosing which opportunities to pursue based on their potential. While my focus right now is on serving my family, I still see coaching in my future. Over the course of nine years, I've developed twenty-four all-league players, participated in five championships (winning two), and coached nine top-ranked defenses. It's quite remarkable for someone with my background to achieve these things. I have proven that coaching is truly my God-given talent. I believe it's a spiritual gift for me to connect with young people, particularly young men, and to serve as a role model and a strongleader. And to think, I never imagined I would be doing all of this from Des Moines, Iowa.

Moving to the Midwest has been a wise decision in many ways. As of now, I believe Des Moines is the best city to live in America. I am certain that God led me here to transform my lifestyle, to redefine my service to Him, to reconsider the importance of faith, to find my wife, and to start afresh in my relationship with Christ. I have been able to make a significant impact on this community. I have worked in various capacities, and I believe that where I am in life right now is an ideal place to continue serving. God brought me to a place that needed diversity, and as an African American, I am here to bring people together. I am a Christian, and I don't adhere to any specific denomination. I enjoy attending Catholic churches as much as Baptist churches. I appreciate Lutheran churches because their pastors are non- judgmental and open to people of all Christian faiths. My journey as a Christian is still ongoing, but living in Iowa has provided me with the opportunity to grow in my faith. I don't have the same negative influences and distractions that I encountered during my professional career, especially when I lived in Toronto, where beauty, nightlife, and constant excitement were abundant, but spirituality was lacking. It was easy to become spiritually derailed in that environment.

Here in Des Moines, my day starts early as I wake up to prepare breakfast for my kids around 7:30 a.m. They have a little bit of free time to get themselves up, brush their teeth, and go through their morning routine. After breakfast, we tackle a few chores and tidy up our rooms and the areas we were playing in. Following that, we have our 10:00 a.m. story time, and at 11:00 a.m., it's sister time, where they spend about an hour playing together. By then, it's time for lunch, and nap time usually falls around 1:00 p.m. After naps, we head to the pool and engage in various activities until around 5:00 p.m. when my wife gets home. That's our usual schedule. During the summer, we drop my daughter off at 9:00 a.m. at Vacation Bible School, which runs for a week. We like sending her to VBS so she can experience a different setting to express her love for God, rather than just being in a structured church classroom setting. Our church is quite large, and VBS caters to about eight and a half thousand kids over two weeks, which is a significant undertaking. This is the same church I'm working with for my faith-based conditioning youth camp. The daily activities and the free time I have now to spend with my family are what led to my decision to step down from my dream job. It has given me the opportunity to be present at home and witness my children growing up, whereas, during my professional career, I was constantly away. I'm sure my children suffered to some extent because I wasn't there, but now I have another chance: a do- over. I married my best friend, and we now have two more daughters who are around the same age, and I have the opportunity to do things better this time around. No amount of money can buy the time and attention I can give them. Right now, I believe that God has placed me exactly where He needs and wants me to be, and I see my family thriving because of it.

Looking back to when I was younger, I realize that I didn't have the same level of confidence that I have now. I wasn't as sure about my approach to family, politics, or religion. I didn't have a clear path to what I wanted to do and who God made me to be. As I've matured, I've gained a better understanding of life situations. I know that the primary reason God put me in this world is to be a family man. Every good thing I've received from God has happened while I've been taking care of my family, including my parents and siblings, as a Christian man should.

I'm in great health, both spiritually and physically. My marriage is in a great place-in many ways, it always has been, but we are growing together as a couple. My kids are also in a healthy space because I am now more involved in their lives instead of being away coaching somewhere. I can see amazing things happening, and I know it's because God has placed me exactly where He wants me.

Living an **iNvincible** life means doing what you are meant to do to the best of your ability, all while honoring God in the process.

Now, I ask you...

Are *you* in the **iNcrowd?**

Are *you* living an **iNcomparable, iNexhaustible, iNfluential, iNspirational, iNvincible** life?

Appendices

Glossary of iNclusions

To me, it means being unmatched, surpassing any form of comparison. In terms of my experiences, professional football was on a different level compared to any other profession or work I had ever done. Transitioning from the urban jungle of DC to Arkansas and then to the countryside of Glasgow, Scotland, while playing football, made my story incomparable to most others. **iNexhaustible:** To me means to be without fatigue; to be relentless, perseverance, drive, sustainability, never quitting, never giving up. My natural athletic ability and drive to be successful made me incomparable to others on the playing field. I achieved and sustained a level of athletic excellence that very few possessed in my ten years of playing and nine years coaching.

iNfluential: To me, this represents the impact we have on others and to the world. I have always been an influential and charismatic person. When I learned how to apply that to leadership, I became an asset and a threat. I had to learn how to influence without intimidation. As a player and coach, I learned to influence others through leadership and example. Dominance, personality, and a strong work ethic are my tools of influence.

iNspirational: To me, this is distinct from influential. To be a true inspiration one must do something above themselves and above what is normally required. My faith is the main inspiration and the tool I use to inspire others. Another inspiration was my career and successes that seemingly came from nowhere.

iNvincible: To me, this represents the inability to be defeated. In my career, I felt invincible for a stretch of time where I was dominating multiple leagues in pursuit of the NFL. I had a covenant with God and I felt that he was protecting me from all my enemies-hence, truly invincible.

About Kahlil Carter

Kahlil Rafiq Carter is a retired professional football player and current professional football coach who has served as Head coach of the Cologne Centurions of the European League of Football, Defensive Coordinator of the Montreal Alouettes, and Secondary Coach for the Calgary Stampeders, both of the Canadian Football League. Coach Carter has also coached at the high school and collegiate levels with West Des Moines Valley High School and Drake University in Iowa.

From 2011-2017 Carter's teams appeared in 5 championships and produced 17 all-league players. Coach S.W.A.A.G. as he has affectionately become known as, also starred in the Arena Football League for 8 teams, played in the Canadian League Toronto and Montreal, and spent time in the NFL with Buffalo as well as Scotland of the NFL Europe. Carter was recognized throughout his career as a journeyman cover cornerback, finishing his career with 50 career interceptions and 9 defensive touchdowns.

Kahlil lives by the acronym SWAAG.

1. Students Working towards Academic and Athletic Goals

2. Serving a Wonderful And Amazing God

3. How you wear your confidence and style

Acknowledgements

I extend my deepest gratitude to Almighty God in Heaven and His beloved son, Jesus Christ, for their unwavering guidance and blessings throughout my journey. Their divine presence has been my constant source of strength and inspiration.

To my loving wife Courtney, your boundless support, understanding, and love have been the cornerstone of my life. I am endlessly grateful for your unwavering commitment and the joy you bring to our family.

A heartfelt appreciation goes out to my four incredible daughters Briana, Brooklyn, Mya, and Belize. Your presence fills my life with joy, and I am blessed to witness your growth and achievements. Each of you is a source of pride and inspiration. To my mother Linda, your love and sacrifices have shaped me into the person I am today. Your unwavering support has been a beacon of light, guiding me through life's twists and turns.

I express my thanks to my brothers Aaron and Randii, whose camaraderie and support have been a constant source of strength and encouragement.

In the realm of coaches, I owe a debt of gratitude to John Jenkins, John Gregory, Jay Gruden, Marc Trestman, Pinball Clemons, Gary Anderson, JT Smith, Rick Frazier, Devone Claybrooks, Hal Dyer, Jack Bicknell, Willie Fears, Mark Stoute, Bob Landsee, and Carl Hargraves. Your mentorship and guidance have been invaluable, shaping my skills and character both on and off the field.

This journey would not have been the same without the expertise and encouragement of coaches who have played pivotal roles in my career, namely Rick Frazier, Devone Claybrooks, Hal Dyer, Jack Bicknell, Willie Fears, Mark Stoute, Bob Landsee, and Carl Hargraves. Your dedication to excellence and belief in my potential has left an indelible mark on my professional growth.

I express my deepest gratitude to each of these remarkable individuals who have touched my life and contributed to my personal and professional development. Your support has been a 134 driving force behind my achievements, and I am truly thankful for the impact you have had on my journey.

Game Plan!

IN ORDER TO SUCCEED IN YOUR PLAN, YOU MUST PLAN TO SUCCEED. PLANNING IS AN ESSENTIAL PART OF A SUCCESSFUL PERSONS EVERYDAY. TO SAY IT ANOTHER WAY FAILING TO PLAN IS THE SAME AS PLANNING TO FAIL. I ENCOURAGE ALL OF YOU ASPIRING PROFESSIONAL ATHLETES, COACHES, RETIRING ATHLETES AND FOR ALL OF THOSE THAT DIDN'T HAVE THE CHANCE TO PURSUE THAT DREAM TO USE THE FOLLOWING PAGES TO PLAN OUT YOUR NEXT 3 YEARS. I USE 3 YEAR PLANS INSTEAD OF 5 YEAR PLANS OR I YEAR PLANS IN ORDER TO MAXIMIZE MY FUTURE AND ADEQUATELY USE THE TOOLS IN MY PRESENT. EACH DAY OF EACH MONTH WRITE DOWN 5 ACTIONABLE GOALS FOR THE DAY OR THE WEEK. THESE GOALS CAN REPEAT DAILY. AT THE END OF THE LAST DAY OF EACH MONTH REFLECT ON THESE GOALS BEFORE MOVING ON TO THE MONTH AND AT THE END OF THE YEAR FILL OUT THE PROGRESS REPORT BEFORE GOING TO THE NEXT YEAR. THIS WILL KEEP YOU ON PACE AND ON POINT WITH ACHIEVING SOME SHORT, MEDIUM, AND LONG RANGE GOALS. I WISH YOU ALL MUCH SUCCESS AND TO ENJOY THE JOURNEY AHEAD. YOU ARE KORE THAN A CONQUEROR AND AS SOON AS YOU CAN PUT A VISION TO YOUR GOALS...SUCCESS IS JUST AROUND THE CORNER. GOD BLESS YOU ALL, GOOD LUCK, AND SEE YOU AT THE TOP!

YEAR 1
January

February

March

April

May

_____

_____

_____

_____

_____

_____

_____

_____

_____

_____

_____

_____

_____

_____

_____

_____

June

July

August

September

October

November

_____

_____

_____

_____

_____

_____

_____

_____

_____

_____

_____

_____

_____

_____

_____

_____

December

_____

_____

_____

_____

_____

_____

_____

_____

_____

_____

_____

_____

_____

_____

_____

_____

_____

Progress Report Year

_____

_____

_____

_____

_____

_____

_____

_____

_____

_____

_____

_____

_____

_____

_____

YEAR 2
January

_____

_____

_____

_____

_____

_____

_____

_____

_____

_____

_____

_____

_____

_____

_____

_____

_____

_____

February

March

April

May

June

July

August

_____
_____
_____
_____
_____
_____
_____
_____
_____
_____
_____
_____
_____
_____
_____
_____
_____

September

October

_____

_____

_____

_____

_____

_____

_____

_____

_____

_____

_____

_____

_____

_____

_____

_____

_____

November

_____

_____

_____

_____

_____

_____

_____

_____

_____

_____

_____

_____

_____

_____

_____

_____

_____

December

_____

_____

_____

_____

_____

_____

_____

_____

_____

_____

_____

_____

_____

_____

_____

_____

_____

Progress Report Year

_____

_____

_____

_____

_____

_____

_____

_____

_____

_____

_____

_____

_____

_____

_____

_____

YEAR 3
January

February

March

_____

_____

_____

_____

_____

_____

_____

_____

_____

_____

_____

_____

_____

_____

_____

_____

_____

_____

_____

April

May

June

July

August

September

_____

_____

_____

_____

_____

_____

_____

_____

_____

_____

_____

_____

_____

_____

_____

_____

_____

_____

October

November

_____

_____

_____

_____

_____

_____

_____

_____

_____

_____

_____

_____

_____

_____

_____

_____

_____

December

_____

_____

_____

_____

_____

_____

_____

_____

_____

_____

_____

_____

_____

_____

_____

_____

_____

_____

Progress Report Year

_____

_____

_____

_____

_____

_____

_____

_____

_____

_____

_____

_____

_____

_____

How to Order Bulk Copies

To book Kahlil Carter for your next team, employee, or leadership meeting, conference, retreat, or convention, to order bulk copies, or to request media interviews:

Website: https:/ / icoachswaag.com/

Email: dbcoachcarter@hotmail.com (You will need a more professional email so people can contact you. Even if you want to use gmail, you can create dbcoachcarter@gmail.com, or something like that)

Phone: (240) 498-II 12 (make sure you have a professional sounding voicemail that invites people to engage, or to book you)

If you're a fan of this book, please tell others...

• Write about (book name) on your blog and social media channels.

• Suggest this book to your friends, family, neighbors, and coworkers.

• Write a positive review on Amazon.com.

• Purchase additional copies for your business or sports team, or to give away as gifts.

• Feature Kahlil on your radio or television broadcast.

111Literary Devices. "Heavy is The Head That Wears The Crown. Origin of Heavy is The Head That Wears The Crown." https://literarydevices.net/heavy-is-the   head-that-wears-the-crown/ (accessed October 24, 2018).

www.ingramcontent.com/pod-product-compliance
Lightning Source LLC
Chambersburg PA
CBHW071439090426
42737CB00011B/1719